Desert Daughter

Nancy Key Roeder

Copyright © 2015 Nancy Key Roeder. All rights reserved under International and Pan-American Copyright Conventions. No part of this book may be reproduced or distributed in any form or by any means, or stored in a data base or retrieval system, without written permission from the author. All rights, including electronic, are reserved by the author and publisher.

ISBN: 978-1-63210-014-6
Library of Congress Control Number: 2015945785

Cover art by Joseph S. Willis
Cover design by Pam Knight

This is a work of fiction. Characters and events are products of the author's imagination.

Plain View Press, LLC
1101 W 34th Street, Suite 404

www.plainviewpress.net
Austin, TX 78705

for Julie

Contents

Prologue   9

Part One

Chapter One: Who Is My Father?   17
Chapter Two: Flesh and Bone   29
Chapter Three: A Father's Memoir   47
Chapter Four: Many Mansions   67
Chapter Five: An Ordinary Day   85
Chapter Six: Rowing Alone   101

Part Two

Chapter Seven: Mood of the Dunes   121
Chapter Eight: Witch's Hair   127
Chapter Nine: A World Shattered   151
Chapter Ten: Journey East   159

Part Three

Chapter Eleven: Going Home   173
Chapter Twelve: "You Are Not My Father"   185
Chapter Thirteen: One Cool Dad   197
Chapter Fourteen: The Place You Go   207
Chapter Fifteen: Letting Go   213

Acknowledgments   223
About the Author   225

Here is the time for the sayable, here is its homeland.
Speak and bear witness. More than ever
the Things that we might experience are vanishing, for
what crowds them out and replaces them is an imageless act.
An act under a shell, which easily cracks open as soon as
the business inside outgrows it and seeks new limits.
Between the hammers our heart
endures, just as the tongue does
between the teeth and, despite that,
still is able to praise.

 Rainer Maria Rilke, from *Duino Elegies and*
  The Sonnets to Orpheus (portion of The Ninth)
  (Translated by Stephen Mitchell)

Prologue

The wilderness and the solitary place shall be glad for them; and the desert shall rejoice, and blossom as the rose.
    —Isaiah 35:1

Once upon a time, before Burma Shave signs vanished from southwestern highways; before ATVs cluttered the desert sand dunes; and before television, smart phones and social media changed lives forever, a married couple lived in the Desert Southwest. The man was tall and thin, with brown wavy hair and twinkling blue eyes; the woman, petite, with hazel eyes concealing a mysterious intelligence. They were both dreamers: he, an impractical sort driven by grandiose visions, she, a mixture of the practical and mystical. They courted and honeymooned at night on the desert as a flood of frosty moonlight washed over them on a lava-strewn landscape, and their afterglow beamed as starlight spilled all around them.

    They were very happy, but they longed for a baby to come into their lives. During the early years of their marriage, they enjoyed watching families of Gambel's quail waddle along in their backyard, reminding them of how much they, too, wanted to create a brood. Waiting for the beginnings of new life turned patience into anxiety, hope into quiet despair.

    Summer months were unbearably hot inside their house, so in the evenings they would haul their mattress outside and sleep under the stars. If a cloud shadow moved across the sky, they might catch the silvery shards of a coming moon. Constellations blazed above, and the man would point to Scorpius, visible best in August from the southwestern state where they lived.

    When fall brought an end to blistering heat, the couple strolled on a path in the desert not far from their home, marveling at the multitudinous expressions of life exploding beneath their feet. In the spring, they donned thick boots and sun-protecting hats and walked amongst a profusion of blue, yellow, red, purple and white wildflowers. Bees buzzed all around, and the scents of the desert filled their joyous beings.

Saguaros rose from the sand, looking like contorted towering statues. As the couple meandered, they sometimes laughed and joked and pushed their elbows outwards, raising their arms skyward to imitate the shapes of the saguaro – water laden cacti pock-marked with holes from invading ravens, woodpeckers and screech owls. In the distance, power lines with metal arms shaped like Navajo *yeii* – benevolent or devil spirits – marched along the desert floor.

The desert gave them the sense of the passage of time, of the ancient past and of their present lives. They knew that they were treading in this dry, hot and dusty place where once a mighty sea covered the land for miles upon end, where dinosaurs fed and fought, and where native peoples practiced spirit worship and discovered ingenious ways to use the many parts of the saguaro and the yucca. Ambling along, this couple took care to avoid scorpions and rattlesnakes. They saw lizards – descendants of dinosaurs that once roamed the land – darting here and there and withered snake skins strewn about, cracked and wrinkled, left behind to parch in the sun. Sometimes they would come across other hikers treading this well-known path, but many times they were alone. Hand in hand, they breathed in pure air and squinted at a blinding blue sky while murmuring about their shared happiness, but also of their sadness at not being able to start a family.

Sometimes visions of lakes appeared, just as travelers in any age, in any desert land, are certain they have seen. If these mirages had been real, if they had knelt to stare into those illusory pools, they might have seen reflections of their own faces and witnessed themselves at a moment in time. These were not the features of enraptured young lovers, or those of crones and aged men, but instead those of man and woman in the prime of life, reflections floating in a watery mirror. Perhaps they could have caught the fragments of ancient visages filled with ambient light from a distant past, when deities had dominated then later faded from the minds of humans – gods and goddesses of every culture, kings and queens of the sun and of the moon. There was sacredness about this space that they sensed but could not fully understand.

The woman was quiet and inward-looking, a poet who expressed her awe of this cactus-covered terrain, so different from the one she knew from her growing up years in the American Midwest. She imagined the desert and the mountain backdrop as the ragged aftermath of lava thrust upward from a giant's mighty heart. The desert at night was a witch-man with thorns for hair and sharp cruel fingers on claw-like hands, weaving a spell with a gossamer thread, luring her into his silken net, capturing her in a web of star-lit beauty and terror, which, perversely, she never wishes to escape.

The man was a restless sort with many interests, someone who always had to be moving, doing, traveling, who became so fascinated with the varieties and beauties of cactus flowers that he became an avid photographer. He started a collection of colored slides to record the fuchsias, golds and creamy whites of the prickly pear, lush ivories and brilliant corals of the barrel cactus, and the lily-like whites of the prodigious saguaro. Also claiming his attention was the ubiquitous ocotillo. When rains came to the desert, it sprouted fiery orange blooms on its ugly, waving stick-like arms. The man took many pictures of this unusual plant, and the woman teased him that the beautiful ocotillo had captured his heart.

But his attraction to the ocotillo could not compare to his fascination with the legend about a mine rich with gold, supposedly hidden in the nearby Superstition Mountains.

Many explorers ventured forth and sought, but some never returned alive. In due time, doubt was cast on the story, but not enough to deter the determined. Each evening at sunset, the mountains glowed golden, reminding new seekers of gold dust and of the mine that was supposed to exist deep inside the rugged and inscrutable mountains. The glint in the man's eye matched the gleam of those sun-struck peaks. He would not attempt to climb Superstition Mountain, he assured her, but he did not doubt that someday he would discover riches and that their lives would be filled with plenitude.

Then one day the woman at last knew that she would bear a child, and her happiness overflowed. But that joy was smothered when the baby girl made its appearance six months later, and at three pounds – this was before advances for tiny newborns – did not survive. The man held a burial service for the child, but he would not allow his wife to be present, believing that she could not handle the grief and stress over this terrible loss.

Within a year, another child began to grow in the woman, but this time she tempered her expectations. The child would be born under the sign of Scorpio, so named for the constellation where, it was imagined long ago, stars outlined the pincers and tail of an insect prevalent in their region. When a healthy baby girl arrived two weeks past the anticipated date, the husband was on a business trip and not present for the birth. But he drove home breaking all speed limits, arriving at the hospital to find his wife beaming, holding their newborn daughter and stroking the baby's soft cheeks, rosy as a desert sunrise.

The man was so proud of his achievement that he, with some literary help from his wife, wrote a clever birth announcement about how they had produced a new amazing product – the father was through and through a salesman – one that should be handled with care, scrubbed well with soap and water and wrapped in cellophane. He mailed out dozens of copies to business associates, clients, friends and family members. He named himself as the chief producer and his wife as the collaborator.

Over time, the father became less enamored of his daughter and more focused on the pursuit of riches. That goal gleamed in his brain, just as it had when he and his bride had lived near the foot of the mountain, which, it was said, held golden treasure. And, when several years later a new baby daughter came to live with the family, the father turned his attention to her, forgetting about his firstborn. Thus it occurred through the years that the once-adored child became an afterthought in her father's mind and heart.

Because of the father's decisions, the family moved numerous times so that he might chase his dreams, a never ending hunt for treasure, an unshakeable belief that he would find his fortune. As the daughter grew into womanhood, she wished for a father who would be aware of her presence, for sometimes it was as if she were invisible to him.

Before, in the desert, the couple had shared a blissful time together. The desert at that time was their Garden of Eden. But, as in all fairy tales, human weakness and the reality of everyday life intruded. Their lives became fraught with strife because the man persisted in his obsession. The woman dutifully bore her choice of a husband. She loved him. He was so unlike her own father whose strict treatment of her had caused resentment and hurt that only escape from her birth family would remedy, but she despaired at her husband's fixation, which precipitated a financial downslide for the entire family. Nevertheless, she would not leave him even though there were times when she thought she might do just that. Her father had been such a trial to her that she had vowed never to marry someone like him. In this, she succeeded, only to exchange one set of problems for another.

The first daughter of the couple, born under the sign of Scorpio, also grew up determined never to marry a person like her father. At first there was happiness, but later that marriage was beset by disappointment when her husband began to taunt and diminish her publicly as her interests grew divergent from his. Their precocious daughter, on whom they lavished all the material blessings that both of them had missed in their childhoods, became used to luxury and demanded more of everything. When the marriage ended, that daughter suffered and pursued choices that would dull her pain. She idolized her father, who fancied his liquor more than he did her, and for many years, she never stopped trying to gain his love.

This is the story of the journeys taken by three women from three generations, all seeking an elusive answer to an age-old question: Who is my father? The fathers in these tales, save one, were not aware of this yearning, nor did they deem it important. Sturdy and self-confident, they believed themselves to live in a world of opportunities, and their preoccupations left little time for such interpersonal matters. In grasping for the gold ring, these men missed the riches that lay before them. Likewise, the women overlooked their inner strength and allowed themselves to be filled with shame and self-loathing. They had to venture out to find successes of their own through choices made and chances taken, both foolish and wise, with hurt coming before healing. They had to step through many brambles before they could emerge from their personal deserts to discover that cactus flowers sprout alongside painful thorns.

Part One

Surely there is a vein for the silver, and a place for the gold where they fine (sic) it.
— Job 28:1

In those days they shall say no more, The fathers have eaten a sour grape, and the children's teeth are set on edge.
— Jeremiah 31:29

Chapter One
Who Is My Father?

June 10, 1991

The driver of the silver Subaru took the off-ramp just north of Denver, turning west off Interstate 25 just before sunset. Quickly lowering the shade to shield her vision from the blinding brightness, she bent to the left along with the car as it looped gracefully onto the ramp leading west to Boulder. If viewed from above, the entire maneuver might have been seen to form a wide half-circle, as if a lariat had been tossed out to capture something that never could quite be caught. And then the rope, if it really were one instead of a stretch of highway, straightened itself out. Ahead lay the Flatirons Mountains, sheer walls of jagged granite with one conspicuous cliff on the north end tipping southward like the prow of a massive ship listing in the ocean, so different from the graceful outline of the Sandias visible to the east in central New Mexico. The Subaru hummed along the asphalt ribbon, moving steadily toward its destination.

Both riders were weary, anxious for the comfort of familiar surroundings, having traveled all day from Albuquerque. As the car now glided onto Highway 36, once known as the Boulder Turnpike, they faced what had been developing outside the left windows but had not yet burst fully into their vision. Now they drew in their collective breath. The sky was pulsing and glowing, and across its vast expanse were shooting stripes of coral and vermillion. It was extraordinary, more shimmering, more blazing than most late spring lemon-orange Colorado sunsets. This evening's dress mode belonged to the mysterious woman at the ball whose entrance in a stunning costume dazzles the revelers, causing them to gasp.

Linda Richardson and her daughter were returning from a whirlwind weekend trip to help Christi retrieve her remaining belongings stashed in a storage locker in Albuquerque during her college years, now completed. Christi was joining throngs of her peers in moving back home before deciding what to do with her life. The other reason for the trip was to visit with Linda's aging parents.

"The sky is putting on such beautiful colors for Granddaddy," Christi remarked. "When he dies, I know he's going to a beautiful heaven."

"He seemed in good spirits, didn't he?" Linda said, shifting in her seat uneasily because she, too, had seen how much her father had slowed down from the last visit just six months before. Well, after all, he was ninety-three.

"But, Mom, you know he's old. Isn't that what happens to older people, that they just die?"

Linda sighed, declining to enter a discussion with Christi about how death doesn't always come that fast when you are old. You sometimes just linger, but you are never as vigorous as your former self, or disease takes you slowly rather than rapidly. And sometimes you're young and get sick or die in some sort of unexpected accident.

"You do believe in heaven, don't you, Mom?" Christi was now twenty-one. In Linda's mind, Christi had rarely shown much interest in religious or spiritual or what-happens-after-life issues. Except for the time the two of them had visited Linda's hometown. But not a word since that trip over ten years ago. Maybe this was some new interest for Christi, a move toward matters deeper than where the nearest mall might be.

Trying to keep her eyes focused on the highway, maneuvering from lane to lane as traffic permitted, Linda thought to herself, No. Yes. Maybe. I don't know. Depends on the definition. Her views were always changing, evolving, complicated. It was not the time to respond, but she did not wish to squelch Christi's curiosity, nor forego an opportunity for them to have a closer relationship.

Avoiding a direct answer, Linda said, "Christi, I would love to talk to you about this, but sometime when I'm not driving." She paused, then spoke again, trying to lighten the tone of this conversation. "I just remembered something you said when you were around seven, when your bunny got stolen from the backyard by – oh, I don't know, probably raccoons, and you asked me, 'When Thumper goes to heaven, will he have a beard?' "

Christi cracked a smile. She had always been the creator of unusual expressions, so cleverly put. Larry had never failed to chuckle at her precocious verbal ability. But beneath it all, Linda had wondered, might Christi be asking a deep and unanswerable question about where we go after we're not here. She wished later that she had not joined Larry, her ex-husband, in laughing it off.

Linda glanced quickly at Christi, whose smile had faded. She sat glumly in the passenger seat, remaining silent. Linda had no idea what her daughter was thinking. Christi did not always share as much as Linda wished. She ran a hand through her short auburn hair, as if stroking her head might somehow tell her brain what to say next.

Taking her eyes briefly off the line of cars she was following, she turned to her jeans-and-T-shirt-clad daughter, seat-belted to Linda's right, and said, "Why don't you get a picture of this gorgeous sunset? It would be a nice memory."

Twirling a blonde lock that finally had grown out from its punk cut several months before, Christi shrugged and unbuckled herself, swiveled around facing the rear and propped herself on her knees. Even with the swaying of the car, she managed to reach over the headrest and locate, then unzip, the duffel bag resting on the back seat.

As the car lurched during a lane change, Christi bounced a bit and lost temporarily what she had been searching for.

"Mom! Don't do that! I almost had it, the camera, and then you…" Christi was adept at the blame game, especially if her mother caused her some inconvenience.

"Look, why don't we just enjoy the sky? These moments don't repeat themselves, and see, it's already starting to fade." Linda's stomach churned. Maybe she was hungry or just wanted her own bed and could not wait to reach home. But she recognized the feeling of getting clutched when trying to deal with Christi, of sensing that she had failed as a mother.

The sun splashed luminescence on the streaks of pinkish clouds, but patches of indigo were crawling at the edges of the palette. Soon, the show would be gone and by the time they got home, slate blue would have taken over the sky, as if somewhere an ethereal artist had brushed over the light-filled firmament with the darker hues of a somber painting stretched on a taut, gigantic canvas.

The car was riding smoothly now, for the traffic had thinned. Christi had now successfully fished out her camera and twisted back to return to the passenger position. Click went the seat-belt. Then click went the new Canon camera. A frame capturing the essence of brilliance, but not the brilliance itself.

Preserve these moments, Christi, Linda thought to herself. They were now approaching the outskirts of Boulder, facing a more subdued sun, softening the sky with a peach-colored haze.

❧

When the phone call came from Linda's mother early the next morning saying that her father had keeled over and was no longer with them, Linda first flashed on Christi's perspicacity, then began to sort out her own emotional response.

What both amazed and dismayed her was that she felt... nothing. No shock, no grief, no weeping. Surely, it must be abnormal to react this way. Regrets over their non-relationship had long since dissolved into an acceptance of her father's *modus operandi*. Tears shed in the past had dried up, dried like sand on the desert. Her mind whirled trying to grasp some picture, not a photograph but a conception of what it meant to be her father's daughter, to formulate an overall image of the man she had once adored, until slowly over time, she found herself ignored in favor of other, more exciting things – UFOs, card readers, silver and copper mines, and the promise of his religion that leading a virtuous life could guarantee his entrance into heaven someday. And when those preoccupations allowed for a modicum of attention to his family, it was the new sister who claimed his eye, not his firstborn daughter.

The truth was that her father – she was taught to call him Daddy – had deserted her, knocking out the underpinnings of a solid sense of who she was or who she might become. She became aware, as all young children do, only in bits and pieces, of his indifference, his lack of care. Not that he left the family as some fathers do, but that he absented himself from her life, which took its own kind of toll on her.

It took Linda many years to characterize that understanding of who she had *not* been to him, the cherished daughter that she had hoped to be. It took many years to acknowledge that he had abandoned her to his whims and preferences – his religiosity, his grandiose dreams about getting rich. And it took many years to forgive him for his focused attention on her younger sister at the expense of herself.

Now, learning of his death, she coped with feeling guilty for being unable to summon remorse. He was her father. *Honor thy father and mother that thy days may be long upon this earth.* That was drummed into her in Sunday school as a child. She agreed with that dictum in general, though she wondered why it had to be done regardless of the circumstances.

Who was her father? Now he was gone, and she was left not knowing him. All that remained were the longings of what might have been but never was.

∽⧽∾

There was a time, before memory had words and before thoughts could be translated into words, when Linda knew on some instinctual level that she had been bathed in baby-love. Whether it was her mother's rocking or her father's enfolding in his arms, she understood that she was protected and cared for.

Just exactly when the loosening of the bond with her father began to happen, she could not be certain, but, like a leaf caught and detached from its limb by a wispy southwestern summer breeze, she drifted away slowly, imperceptibly, until at some point she knew she would never be attached to the branch again, to that half of the tree that had once nurtured her and given her the chance to be alive. The floating away was so subtle, so gradual that it was not noticed until at some point the sting of it was like the March sandstorms, when the desert air whirled with dirt and pummeled her skin.

As she was growing up, Linda puzzled over how to make sense of what drove her father, why other things out there in the world were always more important to him than she was. There was the matter of misplaced priorities that took her years to recognize.

"We have to take care of the widows and orphans," he would say as he dropped coins that he could ill afford into the collection plate on Sunday mornings. People he did not know seemed more important than his own family who were rapidly plummeting into poverty.

Desert Daughter

She wondered whether somewhere embedded in his DNA was the singular desire to discover gold or copper or silver in places he believed that no one else had found. Driven by that goal, he was gone much of the time, operating as a one-man prospector. He missed the irony that true riches, a family who worshipped him, lay under his nose, but perhaps he regarded them as commonplace, expected, taken for granted. The chase provided thrill enough. At one point, he managed to extract enough ore of a certain mineral and ship it by railway car to California on contract, only to be informed that it had arrived jostled to a pile of dust. He shrugged his shoulders, for he believed, truly believed, that the next time would prove more successful. He was undaunted, even in momentary defeat. Looking back on those days, Linda could only imagine her mother's futile attempts to dissuade him from this quest.

The vestiges of hurt feelings lingered, first raw, then later mellowed into a kind of recollection that she put away and tried not to revisit. Surely, he was not as bad as some fathers of friends she knew. But she decided at some point that no one else could measure another person's anger or resentment or disappointment. Justified or not, those emotions were there, deep inside her, affecting her choices in life, making her yearn for what would never be.

Abuse – surely that was one reason why daughters reject their fathers. Linda could recall a few applications of the razor strop on her tender legs when she was young. There were not many, but they were memorable. Her mother had never stopped him. Far more hurtful than the stings was that Linda never understood how she had been so dreadfully disobedient, why she had earned the punishment, or what to do to avoid a repeat. Those sessions served to make her a submissive daughter, fearful of challenging him or speaking up on her own behalf. Or ever, ever displaying the anger she concealed within. She pondered whether, if she had been able to muster the courage to confront him, would she have felt good about herself? Or ashamed that she had dishonored him?

No apologies ever came forth, only occasional hugs from her mother who glanced at her father but said nothing. Sometimes her father even winked at her mother, as if to say he was doing his parental duty. When her parents met eye to eye, Linda felt excluded, dipped in shame.

Alcohol was never part of the picture. Linda had grown up assuming that all families were like hers, where alcohol was evil and smoking was never to be taken up. In his favor, she admitted, was the fact that he was a non-drinker, unlike so many fathers that wreck families by getting hooked on the bottle.

"We're Christians," her parents said, as if being pious and alcohol-abstinent meant the same thing.

Linda learned from her mother that in his early days as a traveling salesman, before Linda was born, his supervisor urged him to cultivate new clients by "going out drinking with the boys." He refused and nearly got himself fired, but he was so effective in his selling that the management retained him. In fact, he was promoted to a sales manager.

Nor was there anything in the way of domestic violence. Never once did Linda observe that he was unkind to her mother. On rare occasions, sarcastic remarks got tossed around, but then he would change his tone and say, "Hey, I really liked that chicken dinner you fixed." And he would grin. It was difficult to tell whether he was offering a compliment on the meal or trying to get back in her mother's good graces.

Her father alternated between sporadic episodes of attention and unexplainable distancing that left her confused and off balance. As she labored to cope with his mercurial behavior, she began to resent that his needs and desires were the only ones that mattered, that he was to be catered to, worshiped and never questioned for his decisions regardless of their effect on the family.

The litany of disregard left its mark. Being there but not being there. Leaving home for days on end to stake mining claims in the desert. Forgetting how old she was, and asking her, unaware of what he was communicating to her. Never giving her a card for her birthday. Cashing in his life insurance policy, which was to be her college fund, to buy mining equipment. Forbidding her to try out for roles in high school plays. Declining to attend her high school graduation ceremony where she was to be honored as valedictorian. Insisting that she needed go to business school to become a secretary, when she wanted to go to college. Never asking about her dreams about what she might become as she grew up, assuming that she would do just what he thought was best. Telling her to get down on her knees and confess her sins to Jesus Christ. Trying to marry her off to the son of an old friend.

That was one of the most egregious of his fantastical ideas. Near the end of her senior year of high school, her father approached her, holding a letter in his hand.

"This is from Jesse. You know, I've mentioned our friends the Camerons, our neighbors when we lived in Tucson. Frank – that's their son. He wants to come and get you and marry you. I think you should write him and accept his offer."

"Oh, Daddy, no! I don't even know him – have never met him!" She had heard enough about him to know that she never would, if she could help it. This man was ten or twelve years older than she, living as a nomad on the Arizona desert drinking goat's milk and tending to his food allergies. What was her father thinking? But her father had never asked what she wanted out of life. He was behaving as if she were some kind of throwback to ancient time or a girl living in a culture that still obeyed their fathers about arranged marriages.

She was beginning to formulate some goals of her own. She wanted to enroll in the university with the scholarship she had been awarded and work toward a degree leading to a teaching career. Another hope was that she might meet someone to marry who would never jeopardize the financial security she so desperately sought. It was an unspoken rule of her generation that the most worthy goal was to become a wife and mother. Full-time careers for women, while considered to be "insurance," always were to be submerged in favor of the husband's. It was not only her mother and peer group who reinforced this model, so did the movies and TV shows.

But what she did not want and would refuse to do was to take up life with a man she had never met. For all she knew, he lived in a tent! She would not have that. For once, her father listened to her protests and dropped the subject.

As she reflected on her life with her father, she realized how simple her desires were. Mostly, to share time with him, to have him ask her what she thought about things, to treat her as person with a curious mind and hopes and dreams. Maybe teach her how to fish or how to work a simple camera. The hard thing was having his presence but not his attention. His eyes were always gleaming, but not at her. He was a constant talker, but it was always *at* her, not *to* her, words spilling out about himself, his opinions, his food needs or about religion. Sometimes along the way she thought it might have been easier if there had been a divorce or if he had gone to the war as some of her friends' fathers had done and had never come back.

✌︎✌︎

Linda's conflicted reactions to her father were at odds with his reputation. He was charismatic. People adored him, his charm, his good looks, his palaver. He was trusted. They plucked him from a crowd as a leader, even asked him at one time if he would run for mayor of the town where Linda spent a good part of her childhood.

Coupled with the outward persona was a strong sense of ethics and morality ingrained from his strict Presbyterian upbringing. He had a compassion for the downtrodden but saw no contradiction in giving away money to people he did not know, while his wife and family scraped by, deprived at times even of grocery money.

Still, he could stretch the rules when it benefited him. Her mother mentioned a time in their early married life when he began to fix the electric meter so that the city reader would gather a figure showing less electricity than actually used. He rationalized his behavior her by saying, "When the utility company robs you blind, you have a right to defend yourself."

As Linda grew to womanhood, she struggled to accept her father's legacy of narcissism, but also his caring and his many contradictions. Her father *did* care about her health and her salvation. He took her to church and to doctors.

Chapter Two
Flesh and Bone

And Adam said, "This is now bone from my bones and flesh of my flesh and she shall be called Woman because she was taken out of Man."
       —Genesis 2:23

June 7, 1991

Linda's brief time with her aging father three days before his death had contained all the predicted and repeated elements of all such visits except for one: an unexpected invitation to go to lunch at his favorite place, a cafeteria featuring down home cooking, the kind her mother fixed during her childhood – pot roast with carrots and onions swimming in gravy, fried chicken dredged in mashed cornflakes, whipped potatoes doused with butter, meatloaf expanded with oatmeal and smothered in ketchup. Her father used to hunt deer with men friends each fall. If a deer was slain, the men divided up the dressed meat and delivered it to the town frozen locker, so sometimes they ate venison. Chicken, with feathers plucked clean after their heads were detached with her father's ax, came from local farmers and ended up on their plates fried or stewed. And then, endless days of chicken soup.

   Their neighbors were descendants of mestizo families that had populated the river valley for centuries. They grew corn and beans and squash, and fixed foods so foreign – nearly everything spiced with red pepper and cumin – that her mother refused to learn their ways, choosing to stay true to the bland fare that both she and her husband, in different parts of the country, grew up with. Salt alone would do for seasoning a roast or fried chicken or ground meat. Her father swore he was allergic to black pepper.

There had been no meals out in restaurants in those early years of Linda's life. No money. Her mother's words, spoken far too many times, were "be resourceful" or "pray" – all because of her father's financial squandering, his inattention to his business, his failure to support the people depending upon him.

"Something will turn up." That was what her father, ever the optimist, would say when things got dire. Linda's mother used to tell her that Henry Perchfield Richardson was like Mr. Macawber in *David Copperfield*, a lovable and charming sort forever throwing the family into debt and ending up in debtor's prison. Except that Henry Richardson never went to prison, just managed to create a restrictive life for those depending upon him for support. What turned up was usually another idea about how to strike it rich.

But what turned up this time was her father's surprise offer. She agreed to it readily. Her father could no longer hop into his car and peel off to God knows where, but he still showed remarkable flexibility in maneuvering in and out of the automobile. His favorite activity was driving. Linda once wrote a poem about him, entitling it "The Travelin' Man." Restless, always on the move, that was her father.

Walking to the car, Linda noticed him tightening his belt so much that his pants puckered. Excess weight had never plagued him, but now his figure was taking on the look of a scarecrow. He had never been toweringly tall, but now was a diminished, thinly grayed version of the handsome, wavy-haired man with the clipped moustache – the one who had constructed a swing for her when she was four, bought her a bicycle when she was eight, and taught her to drive at age sixteen. Those were pleasant things to remember about her father. But the years spaced between these offerings had been marked by his treatment of her as a non-person.

The cafeteria was in a strip mall, not far from her parents' home. It was too much to hope that he would ask where she might like to go, possibly a salad place. She knew better than to suggest an alternative. Long ago she understood that he would be the one to dictate the terms of their relationship and that he would be oblivious to the fact that his behavior should be any different. Most likely, the thought that she might have a preference for a different restaurant never entered his mind.

Linda was certain that her father never doubted himself or his capabilities. But still, she had to wonder if somehow, toward the end of his life, a glimmer of knowledge had seeped through the layers of complete self-assurance. She sensed that he might feel this was his way of making up for the never-to-be-reclaimed years during which she was the forgotten child. Or maybe her mother was behind it all. Linda never knew what they discussed, for they kept their conversations private. She wanted to believe that this lunch was some kind of offering of his repentance, his unspoken gesture of asking for forgiveness.

A wave of 100-degree dry air spurred them to hustle across the asphalt parking lot as quickly as possible. Linda noticed her father's forehead drenched in perspiration. She worried that he was too old to be going out in this heat.

Relief arrived as they pushed the brass handles, opening the oak doors to welcome a blast of refrigerated air conditioning. The cafeteria's homey atmosphere sported oak wainscoting with turquoise and white plaid wallpaper above, chairs upholstered in vinyl stamped with a design of faded roses and verdant leaves, and tabletops of cream-colored Formica bordered in faux wood. The scents were pleasant, reminding customers of comfort food.

Linda picked up her tray and followed behind her father, where they joined a long line of customers eyeing an array of bowls of salads, sherbet dishes glistening with cubes of wiggly Jell-O, plates of pie wedges and gooey cake slices, all roosting on crushed ice behind a slanted glass enclosure open at the top. She reached for a small plate of sliced tomatoes and followed her father down the line. Attendants clad in white aprons shoveled entrées and side dishes onto beige crockery plates edged with a deep brown circle. They smiled, wielding spatulas with expertise, but did not allow anyone to tarry. "Potatoes? Gravy? Chicken-fried steak?"

The grilled chicken looked acceptable, so she asked for a small piece along with some green beans that somehow had escaped from becoming pale. They floated like miniature green boats in buttery juice. Her father chose the same vegetable along with a shrunken hamburger, puréed butternut squash and a baked potato with two pats of foil-wrapped butter.

Sliding her tray over the metal tubing toward the check stand, Linda let her father pay the bill. He was old-fashioned and courtly and took much pride in doing what he considered were gentlemanly things. She recalled images of her father tipping his felt hat to women, holding open a door, walking on the outside portion of the sidewalk. She appreciated these gestures, yet found them at odds with her unresolved memories of personal abandonment. He was friendly with and acknowledged everyone he encountered except her.

They found a table in as quiet a corner as possible. There was a long silence as they focused on eating. Linda winced at the familiar chomping sound. Her father had a way of asserting himself into whatever space he held, wherever that was. For some reason, apparently ignoring urgings from her mother, he had never learned to chew with his mouth closed.

"Well, about these allergies of mine," he said, as if she had not heard this story before. "This is a place where I can get some of the same things that Mother cooks so well for me. Now, of course, her cooking is better, but I didn't want to burden her fixing too many meals while you were here. She's at home right now preparing our supper. You know, these days she gets so agitated and flustered when she has visitors."

Growing up, Linda had never noticed that he always addressed his wife as "Mother." Now she found it extremely odd.

Linda was hit with a familiar wave of uncertainty about her father. She never could grasp precisely what he was implying. Was he trying to make her feel guilty? Or congratulating himself on helping out her mother? Or had her mother prevailed upon him to arrange this luncheon date? There were mysteries of family dynamics that Linda had never been able to solve.

※

"This chicken, uh, tastes fine," Linda said, hesitating, hoping they could turn the conversation corner. She wished that she had picked another topic. Inwardly, she shuddered, recalling how her parents were overly concerned about the effects of certain foods on one's digestive system.

When she was about four, her parents insisted that she, like her father, was allergic to sugar. Her parents banned anything containing it. They warned her harshly. When she was four, she turned down a piece of cake at a neighbor's house to avoid a scolding from her all-powerful parents and evade a session with "the tonic" – castor oil, forced on her when they knew that she had eaten what they deemed to be an offending food.

The food culprits changed, without explanation. The sugar restriction faded away by the time Linda was six, when her mother allowed her to slurp a first-ever strawberry ice cream cone to celebrate the end of sugar rationing during the war years. Later they decided it was egg yolks that "hurt her" along with whole wheat and peanut butter. But absolutely no evidence existed to suggest any problem. She was thirty before she dared test eating an egg. Nothing happened. All was well. She did not get ill. They were wrong.

Some of Linda's earliest memories centered on those odd food obsessions. There were certain things to be avoided, others to be consumed daily. As her parents aged, these beliefs hardened into gospel truths and translated into daily rituals. Her father refused fruit but enjoyed all kinds of cooked vegetables. Her mother, on the other hand, held a firm belief that her stomach troubles were related to vegetables. In recent years she had adhered to a monotonous diet of beef patties, baked potatoes and canned peaches. She prided herself on being the dietary caretaker, the keeper of keys to their health. Once she had enjoyed puttering in her garden, reading the newspaper and favorite books, and writing poetry but now spent most of her time planning and preparing six meals per day – two each for breakfast, lunch and supper.

Linda grieved that her mother, the wide reader, the poet, the planter of irises and roses, had no time now for these activities. She wondered if this fixation with diet gave her mother some control over her husband, who had dominated her for so long. Ironically, her father thrived, exuding energy, while her mother's health declined.

Maybe I'm selling them short, thought Linda. Perhaps they were right. After all, more and more research was being done in the field of nutrition. Still, how could those chronic doses of castor oil be good for you? The problem was that her mother carried things to an extreme. Surely, her father's health had not been harmed by his avoiding sugar. But Linda had suspected for some time that either her mother had an eating disorder or, at the very least, was being starved of vital nutrients by insisting on such a limited diet.

Interrupting her thoughts, her father looked straight at her and winked, those blue eyes sparkling as they always had. That wink had been delivered when she would proudly hand her early school papers with A's on them, or her first clumsily written poems. He would toss his head, flick one eye closed and pull his face to one side in a crooked smile.

Not exactly a beaming smile, but not a frown or a smirk, either, just enough of a characteristic look to put her off balance. She did not know whether this repeated gesture was a sign of admiration or of dismissal.

"I have some things I want to give you when we get home," he said. She could tell that this was something important to him. "I think you should know some things about me, and I want you to have them. After all, you are my daughter, bone of my bone and flesh of my flesh."

Linda knew that the Genesis quote alluded to "Woman" being made as a mate for man. Didn't her father know that, too? Was he implying that the Biblical reference instead was to the offspring that he had been responsible for creating?

Although lately her father tried to be more attentive when she was in his presence, it came as a complete shock that she actually had entered her father's thoughts. Yes, her father had given her life. But did all fathers take pride in that fact alone and then proceed to ignore the growing human being they have caused to come into existence? She had wished for something more in the world outside the womb, something more to validate her existence than the mere fact of the spark between sperm and egg. She was stunned to be anointed the recipient of her father's recorded memories.

"You surprised me," she said, managing a slight smile. Her father returned his famous grin. Having finished their meal, they left their trays on the table and proceeded toward the door.

On her way out, Linda plucked a lemon drop from a dish sitting near the checkout stand, a perk offered as a favor to keep customers returning. Walking to the car, she felt the dry heat of early June rise up in waves and parch her lips. She slid the lemon drop underneath her tongue.

Once they arrived back home, she kissed her mother on the cheek, noticing how tiny she looked standing at the sink in her kitchen, scrubbing potatoes to put in the oven.

"Daddy and I had a nice lunch," she ventured to say to her mother. "But now I have to pack."

Her mother smiled, displaying the familiar visage that made Linda feel that something was being held back. Linda knew that much more was going on in her mother's mind than would ever be divulged. Attempting to divine the inner workings of her mother's brain was as much a chore as trying to understand her father.

"It's so hot today, Mother. Have you thought about using the microwave for the potatoes?" Linda ventured, knowing what the answer would be. Her mother had certain ways of doing things, never to be altered. She was in her late eighties, but still mentally sharp. Maybe caretaking was the answer to longevity. That's what her mother's life was now – taking care of Henry Perchfield Richardson.

"You know I'm not a microwave user," her mother replied. "I wish I could tear the thing out. This place came with it built in. But I'm glad for our air conditioning – first time in my life."

Linda paused wondering about the irony in her mother's statement. The air had not been turned on, and the house was stifling even though it was shaded well by leafy elms and sycamores. She guessed that older people must stay cooler than the outside temperature might dictate. She wondered how high they must have turned up the thermostat in the winter.

As always, her mother was a puzzle. Another smile. Another enigmatic look at Linda, which said that more lay behind the comment than its surface meaning.

"Where's Christi?" asked Linda.

"I was about to tell you. She wanted to see one of her friends," her mother said, "so I explained where to catch the bus at the end of the corner. Her friend would pick her up at the bus stop. But she said she would be home for our dinner, and that her friend would drive her home."

The aroma of a roast, cooking slowly in the Crock-Pot, tantalized Linda's senses. It would be the simple but substantial meal that her mother had always fixed. She was grateful she had eaten lightly at lunch.

The galley kitchen was modest with the colors popular in the 1960s – yellow Formica countertops and an avocado green refrigerator. Oak cabinets lined the walls, while gold and green plaid wallpaper covered the space above them up to the ceiling. Her mother must have thought of this as luxurious, a far cry from the deprivations of her rural childhood and the skimpy, bare-bones kitchens in the houses during her marriage that Linda remembered all too well. But her mother had never complained, and Linda always wondered how she could maintain her spirits.

Christi did return, all smiles, in time to freshen up. Linda was relieved since her daughter's moods tended to swing radically, and sometimes they did not bode for a pleasant time. But Christi put on the appearance of an attentive guest, and dinner time went relatively smoothly. Accompanying the meat was a small salad, freshly baked bread – her mother's specialty – and homemade applesauce for dessert. Of course, her father would not partake of that.

The four of them sat around the maple table in the small eating area. Efforts were put forth, yet Linda felt the palpable strain of not knowing what to talk about. Her mother tried hard to include everyone in the conversation, sending cautionary looks at her husband whenever he veered off into his favorite topics, which usually were about himself or some far out opinions on the state of the world.

Christi volunteered to clean up the dishes. Linda flashed a glance of appreciation, noticing how tired her mother looked. At one time, her mother said she had to watch her weight. At this point, she did not even fill out her dress. Her small frame was slightly stooped. Linda realized then what an effort it had been for her mother to prepare this meal, and she recalled what her father had mentioned this afternoon at the cafeteria.

Dizziness overwhelmed her as thoughts spilled over one another, churning around in her brain. Oddly, she had never before thought that the time might come when one or both of her parents might not be able to take care of themselves. The idea that one would be left without the other to depend upon had never penetrated, until now. Both of them always appeared so vigorous in spite of their digestion problems, which, to Linda's way of thinking, were self-made. But that could happen, she could see that now.

She had fled New Mexico as soon as she could, hoping to escape her past. What stayed was a mix of nostalgia together with an unforgettable sense of brooding that could not be shaken even with the passing years. Once, she had believed that nothing would ever change, that she would always be a little girl immersed in the present, and that there would never be a growing-up time. She could not even imagine that her parents would someday become elderly, and that she herself would grow into middle age and at some point, be old.

✥

After dinner her father said, "Let's go out for a while on the back patio." Another invitation. Would there be more surprises?

In her youth, she had spent many summer evenings with friends, sitting on her front steps. The air hummed with June bugs rattling, winging toward porches and sometimes crawling inside the glass cover over the light bulb only to sizzle themselves to a crisp. Now that her father had suggested sitting outside on the patio to enjoy the cooler temperatures of the evening, would there still be June bugs?

The outdoor veranda, located on the east side facing the massive Sandia mountain range, was sheltered from the blistering sun now setting behind the volcanoes to the west. For a brief while, the mountains glowed pink, then faded to a smudged gray. A breeze rustled the sycamore leaves, cooling the air from the torrid heat of the day. This would be the perfect place to hear about the "items." The only sounds were an occasional automobile accelerating on the street in front of their home.

Depositing herself on a comfortable lounge chair, Linda waited in silence, biding her time, restraining her desire to say something, anything, but knowing that her father had other things to talk about before releasing what was left of his recorded life. She knew what was coming. His two favorite subjects were intertwined – his religious beliefs and predictions for world turmoil. Her mother had talked to him many times about not boring their guests. But she was not a guest to him. She was family, his daughter.

"I look for the next few years to be terrible for the world," he began. "I have predicted for a long time that Am-ur-ica will be punished for her widespread immorality and disrespect for the Creator, the Almighty God, our spiritual and physical Father. I think we're in for at least ten years of hell, but I do not think for one minute that our country will be wiped out of the picture by nuclear warfare, even though the Bible predicts such a holocaust for many nations."

He had always believed himself to have the gift of extrasensory perception inherited from his mother. UFOs were real, from distant planets. He believed the stories that aliens had been aboard an unidentified object that crashed near Roswell in 1948 and that the government had covered up the truth. Card readers offered predictions, but so did the Book of Revelation. He saw no contradiction in his views or any lack of logic by considering multiple sources.

What was he reading these days? Linda wondered about that.

"We might get some missiles, but those who believe in and live by the Ten Commandments will be saved, just like the Jews were saved on many occasions in the last thousand years."

"But the Jews have not always been saved. They've suffered mightily throughout history, Daddy," Linda said, in a rare contradiction to her father's statement. She pointed out that the worst affliction happened during her childhood, although she, like most Americans, did not learn of the shocking happenings in Europe until after the war was over.

He chose to ignore that she disputed his claim about the Jews and did not talk her down as he used to do before she moved away and developed her own views and values. For years she had held out a sliver of hope that they might engage in a reasoned discourse, but she had never found the right words, the successful communication style to affirm *him* but not his beliefs.

As she sat with him now, her mind wandered, transporting her back to the time when he could keep them all captive with his pronouncements. Family mealtimes had meant listening attentively while her father pontificated in long, tedious monologues, anything from the predictions of the Biblical book of Revelation to the perceived Communists in the U.S. government. He thought Joseph McCarthy was a hero.

"He really exposed those Commies," he had said authoritatively. He never mentioned that McCarthy was eventually censured by the United States Senate. Linda had been an early teenager then, not particularly interested in politics or world affairs.

His words rolled over her like a train. There was no stopping their thrust, their force. The memory of those times at the dinner table washed over her, the feeling of being mute, of not being able to speak up to counter the certitude of his beliefs for fear of being humiliated and put down for disagreeing with his claims.

At these family meals, rarely did her mother volunteer her own commentary. Linda's younger sister simply fidgeted.

When Linda grew in awareness of history and culture and wanted to challenge his pronouncements or discuss an alternate view, her father would cut off her words, making her feel tongue-tied. She realized that her own feeble attempts to counteract her father's assertions needed more evidence. She determined to learn more, to read more, to do more research. Then, perhaps she'd have the confidence to bring to the table some backing from an authority. But she also understood that no amount of evidence or examined opinions would satisfy him.

In the role of superb salesman, her father gave the customer no reason to do anything but approve the product. The sales job directed toward her produced a lasting dread of speaking up. She had shrunk from participating in class discussions in college classes, and she had allowed herself to be bullied and verbally attacked by Larry. Looking back, she regretted how much she had permitted herself to be stripped of her own voice.

As her father droned on about his predictions, she remembered when she was in high school and left Faulkner's *The Sound and the Fury* lying on the coffee table. She was more careless in those days, but she should have known. He had picked it up, apparently scanned some of it and scolded her for reading such filthy trash.

"But Daddy, it's for a book report – I didn't…" There wasn't anything he could do about it, but he had made his point. No more laxity, she told herself, in leaving books around where he could see what she was reading.

Then there was the time when she wanted to try out for the high school play in her junior year because she had been sought after by the drama instructor, but she first had to ask permission from her parents.

"Absolutely not," her father had said. "I don't want you associating with anything to do with plays or dramatic productions. It will lead you away from the Christian path."

She had been more than disappointed, seething inwardly with hurt and rage that she dared not express openly. To cross him was to risk being confined to her home, unable to see friends. At that time, she recalled, they called it "being campused." What was so wrong, so immoral about an innocent high school play? Her mother, sympathetic, apologized. Her mother was always making excuses for her father.

Out of his presence, she told Linda, "I think he got this from his mother, who was English. You probably know that at one time, oh, I think around Shakespeare's time, that the theater districts were filled with all sorts of bad people like prostitutes and pickpockets. Traveling actors came to towns and sometimes were allowed to perform their plays, but they were looked down on as unworthy people. And I suppose those prejudices just lasted. And your grandmother was, oh, so, so religious and I guess maybe prudish."

The next year, without asking, Linda auditioned for the senior play and was picked for the lead role. She did not ask her father's permission. Her father refused to attend, but her mother came to celebrate her performance. The review in the local paper the next day cited her acting as "superior."

୶୨୧ଡ଼

Dusk was settling into darkness. Linda wrapped her arms around herself, feeling as desolate now as she had many years ago. She wanted to find some connection, some point of camaraderie, of mutuality between them. She was so different from him, or was she?

From her mother, she had inherited a pragmatic streak, a tendency to be both systematic and reflective, but also susceptible to straying off course when circumstances overwhelmed her. To survive, she had suppressed another part of her personality: visionary, creative and at times, impulsive. Just like her father.

Would he have loved her more, paid more attention had she been…what? Spunkier? Prettier? More vivacious and adventuresome, like her younger sister? Or, dreaded thought that it was, maybe he would have preferred a boy. Since she did not have a brother, Linda did not know how it would have been for her to have another male in the household. Possibly things would have been no better, or maybe worse. She had hoped to have a brother with whom she could play, someone who would buffer her against the strictness of both parents. But she had found too many times that her dreams dissolved into harsh reality.

≈≈

Now her father moved on to an oft-repeated theme, expressing certainty that when he "went," as he put it, that he would be taken up in a chariot to heaven in a blaze of glory because he was a Christian. He was making less and less sense. Or, in his colorful way, was he predicting his coming demise? Certainly, his imagination was flourishing, but was it sliding into craziness? Chariots. Blazes of glory. Really? Did he envision himself as some kind of Old Testament prophet like Ezekiel with his visions of wheels and cherubim rising to the sky?

"Mark my word," he intoned in a strong voice with only an occasional crackle, his gnarled index finger pointing directly at Linda, "your mother and I will be together after we leave this earth. She's gonna go up in that chariot, too."

Linda sat in stunned silence, wondering if paranoia or dementia or both had overtaken her father's brain. But why should she be surprised? In earlier letters from him, he had expressed such thoughts for a long time, but now they came across as even more extreme. She knew that he always was a bit eccentric. Now his inscrutable fascination with UFOs had morphed into something even weirder.

Smother a smile or shed a tear? Her father was utterly certain of his rectitude. His outward journey had been toward earthly riches; later in life he believed he was moving toward something extraterrestrial.

"And when we are both gone, I want you to be sure to watch the house because vandals will invade it. So, for one thing, be sure to lock it up and keep checking on it, because otherwise it will get trashed!"

Imagining herself as the anointed caretaker of their current abode, she smiled to herself with unspoken bemusement about the contraption he had erected in their garage to distill water "because you can't trust the water we drink. It's full of metals and poisons." Well, he should know after all those mining ventures what could happen when extracted minerals leached into the ground water.

And the cases of castor oil, their all-time remedy. What to do with them? Gratefully, she remembered the savory, sweet-sour tang of this afternoon's lemon drop chosen in order to eradicate the memory of the many doses of that vile purgative she had endured as a child.

Linda shifted in her lounge chair, becoming increasingly uncomfortable with the turn the conversation was taking. She wanted to ask, "Where are you getting these ideas? Have you ever thought that I might have a different way of looking at things?" However, long ago she had abandoned any attempt to explain where she had come to in spiritual matters. She gathered her thoughts so she might be able to put things delicately, then spoke up in general terms, hoping he might take the hint.

"I think I understand what you believe and what you want. People of other faiths have their own ways of thinking about these things."

"Well, I suppose that's so. And they can't all be wrong." He looked at her with a bit of a smile.

Linda raised her eyebrows at him. She had expected his words to come out as "they can't all be right." This would have been his way of saying that his way was the correct one. Perhaps she had underestimated her father.

She'd had early exposure to two forms of religion different from her own, a benign form of mainline Protestantism. Her Mexican-American playmates were all Catholic and prayed to the Virgin Mary. They spoke of mortal sins and venial sins and purgatory, and that they could not eat meat on Friday. Although Linda could not understand the reason for the Friday abstinence from meat, she accepted their beliefs with a shrug of her shoulders.

Her friend Rosalie Stone, whose father was a Baptist minister, once took her to a Sunday evening service. She had come home frightened, telling her mother how Rev. Stone screamed at everyone about repenting and becoming saved. Her mother, not Rev. Stone, was the rescuer in this instance. She forbade any more visits to Rosalie's church. Only after attaining adulthood and taking college courses in comparative religion and mythology did she become aware of the immense diversity of spiritual practices and beliefs. For once, she saw that her father had nailed it correctly. They can't all be wrong.

※※

Adept at starting a conversation on politics, then moving to his personal religious beliefs, he now returned to the theme of our country and its wicked ways. "Because Am-ur-i-ca is in for it, you know. Our immoral ways, the devil has invaded us. We will be punished for not following the Ten Commandments. But Christ will take up the saved, you mark my word." There it was, again, that phrase.

When she was a teenager, her father had once admonished her to get down on her knees and confess her sins to Jesus Christ, but he never had gone so far as to demand that she do it right then and there. Just enough urging to produce guilt if she did not perform. But she had a choice in this one. No, Daddy. Not that she believed she was perfect – her mother let her know that in not-so-subtle ways almost every day. But sin in the sense of transgressing God's will, how could she hope to know what that was? Even in her youth, she became determined not to let her father's interpretation of God's will prevail. "Mark my word, daughter, you will regret it if you do not cleanse your soul of your sins."

One meaning of "sin," she knew, was "missing the mark." Well, she was not the only one in the household guilty of that offense. Much later, her mother told her that she had taken him aside and told him, "If you want your daughter to hate you, just keep putting that sort of pressure on her."

If only he had realized that his approach to religion had led her to doubt her faith, to wonder whether there ever was a Father-God if He ignored his children while at the same time demanding strict obedience.

※

The once-apricot sky had now melted from azure to cobalt through stages of slate gray, and city lights were poking holes in the inky black sky. The air temperature was dropping precipitously as the sycamore leaves whooshed, leaving secrets to be pondered.

"Shall we go in now?" Linda asked. "How about those things you wanted to give me?"

Chapter Three
A Father's Memoir

Every man's memory is his private literature.
— Aldous Huxley

Linda retreated to the extra bedroom with the twin beds where she and Christi were staying. She pulled out her suitcase from the closet. They planned to leave around noon the next day, which meant that the eight-hour drive would put them home just before dark.

Her father had presented her with the cardboard box containing the things he wanted her to have. Now was the time to open it, to discover what he deemed important about his life. She began to thumb through the contents, an odd assortment of letters, photos of family members dating back to the early 1900s, a letter written to a sister about his early years, also a thick non-descript bunch of paper folded in thirds.

Prominent in this stash was an X-ray that her father must have taken during his World War I service as a medical technician on a naval hospital ship. She held up the X-ray to get a better view and saw what looked to be either a nail or a piece of shrapnel in a wounded navy seaman's lung. What was the story there? She would have to ask him about that in the morning. There also was a faded black and white photograph of him standing by an early X-ray machine towering over the patient. She could see how her father's hobby and current profession, photography, came from the early experience in the Navy.

It occurred to her that his affinity for card readers and Biblical prophecies were linked in some way to the X-ray machine, a way to "see through" what appears superficially to our limited surface vision. She had tried to make peace with his many oddities, and what stole over her now was a guarded admiration for the way he wished to peer through to the crux of things, however skewed and quirky his opinions and behavior. Perhaps she had discovered an unacknowledged and unbidden gift, her impulse to "see within," to know who, really, her father was.

She found a college essay he wrote at the University of Texas describing how, after the experience gained in the Navy, he wanted to become a roentgenologist, as radiologists once were called, named after Wilhelm Röntgen, the discoverer of X-rays. But he wrote that he gave up the idea. Finances, no doubt, played a role, but he would have been too proud to admit that impediment. Linda knew bits and pieces of the family history – that her grandfather's bad choices and later illnesses had brought a crushing economic blow to their family.

Sitting on the edge of the twin bed, its brown chenille spread rumpled and covered with the contents of the box, Linda lifted her eyes from the cascade of papers and stared ahead blankly. Then she turned back to the task and sifted through more photos. No pictures included her, yet there were several of him and her mother together. Everything in the box was all about him.

As she carefully spread out the documents, her heart began to thump and her palms grew sweaty. The letters, the folded slick pages. Would they say something about her? Here she was, a grown up woman, and yet she retained a primitive hope that she might find some concrete evidence that he cared for her enough to make mention of her as his child, his daughter. Although she had no such expectation, she surprised herself that the old craving for being recognized should still nag at her.

Out fluttered some newspaper clippings from the mid 1940s. Her father's distinct handwriting marked them as having appeared in the local newspaper. There was her father's name, Henry Perchfield Richardson, naming him as a fundraiser in his work through the Chamber of Commerce to purchase land to establish a factory and thus bring in badly needed jobs to the community. Another one mentioned that he had become superintendent of the local Sunday school at the non-denominational Christian church. Yet another was about his installation as president of the Rotary Club. Linda marveled at what was considered "news" at that time.

Now she picked up the set of pages, handwritten on slick paper, the words almost faded but still legible. Dated in 1977, it appeared to be a letter, or a draft, addressed to his youngest sister who was born when he was fifteen. She apparently had asked for his memories of growing up in Texas since she had come along as the final child, so much later than her brother. Linda set it down amidst the clutter on the bed. Emotions were sloshing over her as if someone had dumped a bucket of water on her head.

Setting aside the handwritten memoir, she perused several other letters, all typed on onion-skin, all dated in 1987. One was addressed to the sister of a cousin, responding to learning of that cousin's passing six months before and offering condolences. He opened this letter by apologizing for not knowing this and writing that he had "a strong E.S.P. urge last summer to call him," but "other priorities interfered." He wrote about how close he was to his cousin. It struck Linda that time and circumstance had moved these two cousins far apart, yet neither had kept in touch. Life moved on, and one forgot one's kin. Perhaps self-absorption ran rampant in this family. Maybe she was not the only one who got overlooked.

Now she folded out the thick pieces of paper that comprised the memoir. The handwriting, while faded, was clearly that of her father. With thumb and middle finger, she flicked off some dust before opening and smoothing out the pages.

Nancy Key Roeder

Henry Perchfield Richardson's story

From what I have learned about my origins, I know that the first ancestor to come to the United States arrived in 1777 (just after the Declaration of Independence) from Scotland and settled in North Carolina. Different branches of the family lived there and in Tennessee, while the largest group from which I'm descended ended up in Alabama. My great grandfather and his brother were in the mercantile business in Mobile in the early 1800s. This brother brought his immediate family along with several slaves to Texas in the 1850s, settling near Waco. He secured a total of 2000 acres of Brazos River bottomland, fine for cotton and vegetable farming, which he divided into four-acre lots. Among other things, he established a Presbyterian church in the community. He was a strict churchgoer and specified that if ever anyone sold liquor on any part of the land he owned, that the land would revert back to his estate.

So her heritage included the abomination of slavery. She bowed her head, ashamed to learn of this. Did that explain why her father had marched in the mid 1920s in Texas with the Ku Klux Klan? She remembered how shocked she was when her mother revealed that bit of ignominious history of her father's past. There was an ironic contradiction in the beliefs about the evils of alcohol, but not the horrors of racial prejudice.

Eventually, my grandfather arrived in Texas from Alabama and settled on one of the parcels that my great-uncle had laid out near Waco. This is where my father was born, his brother having been born in Mobile before the move. Once my father and uncle were grown with families of their own, these two brothers decided to search out land to establish a cattle ranch. This was a time when cheap land was available in the Indian Territory in what is now the state of Oklahoma, so the purchase was made. My uncle went first in 1898 to build his home and ours as well as digging the required wells for each home. My own family stayed behind, as did my uncle's wife. Mother was pregnant with me, in very poor health and upset emotionally about the prospect of moving. She bordered on what might be called today a nervous breakdown. After I was born, I did rather poorly (healthwise). Fortunately, my aunt was on hand to nurse me, literally, along with her child (my cousin) who had been born six weeks before me, making the two of us growing up very close. In fact, if it hadn't been for my aunt's care during those first few months of my life, I probably would not be around to write this.

My aunt was a gifted healer. She could prescribe for almost anything that occurred in the way of sickness, and with her magic touch could heal all the problems kids have. She was elected "the doctor" for all of the children of the two families – and we all loved her very much. Anyway, Mother's health did seem gradually to improve, and we prepared to move to the Chickasaw Nation.[1]

My mother had the gift of E.S.P. – extra sensory perception – which proved to be correct with the fulfillment of a tragedy which happened a couple of years after we got settled in our new place. She saw a dark cloud hanging over this area even before we moved there. But nothing could stop the move at that point, so move we did in 1899, of course, in covered wagons.

My own recollection of events began in 1902 when I was four years old. The Territory was settling up fast with legitimate and illegitimate land holders. The ones who were there first were called squatters and other names

---

1 Historical note: The Chickasaw Nation was created after the Chickasaw people were forcibly removed by the US Federal government to Indian Territory in the 1830s. In 1893, the Dawes Commission was authorized to convince several Indian tribes to cede tribal title of Indian lands and adopt the policy of dividing tribal lands into individual allotments. The US government then sold surplus land to American and immigrant settlers from these allotments, and sometimes the Indians themselves did this.

not suitable for printing. For the most part the squatters treated any newcomers into the territory as "unwanted" or "undesirables."

At this time the family consisted of six – Mother, Dad, my older brother and two older sisters, so I was the baby of the family. One unforgettable night everyone was awakened by a series of commotions outside, so Dad loaded the trusty double barrel shotgun hurriedly and by this time we could see out our windows that our large stacks (or "ricks") of alfalfa hay were on fire.

The horses in the corral were snorting and rearing up on their hind legs and making all the noise that a horse can make. Our milk cows were in an adjoining corral. The corrals were built out of oak posts and were already starting to burn, so we formed a bucket brigade from the well to the burning corral fence in a mighty but too late effort to free the horses. The heat from the two large alfalfa stacks was so fierce we could not save the horses. The half-breed Indians (known as squatters, because they were the first in the territory and had inter-married with the various Native American women there) hated newcomers like us and had thrown cans of coal oil (kerosene) and torched the two stacks of alfalfa, which were very close to our horse pens.

The loss of all the horses and cows was the signal for Dad to say, "The squatters can have it. I don't want it anymore. I'm going back to Texas where there's some law and order!" Unbelievably, my uncle's family did not know till the next day after the fire that anything had happened (they lived about a mile away) because there were no phones in those days.

Soon after this terrible tragedy, which I witnessed and many times have seen again and again in my mind's eye, Dad and his brother (who lived a couple of miles away on an adjoining ranch) borrowed a couple of saddle horses and rode over into Texas looking for another ranch. They found what they were looking for in Hansford County, Texas. A fresh water creek (the Palo Duro) ran through the middle of the property, even though most of the 700 acres of my Dad's portion was up on the top of the cap rock and was as flat as a pancake. The brothers again divided the property up with adjoining homes. As we settled into our respective new homes, my uncle started his flock of sheep that he had wanted for so many years.

My cousin and I were just the right age to become sheep herders. He was six weeks older and usually got the assignment of herding the sheep, so of course I begged to help him. Our job was to protect the sheep from coyotes. We had to avoid the many rattlesnakes that inhabited the area and deal with the many colonies of prairie dogs. We spent hours perfecting our sling shots and tried to kill with small rocks these agile little rascals. Sometimes it was the only recreation we had all day long – that and digging for arrowhead flints. One day we discovered a gallon bucket full of arrowheads and one tomahawk head. How I wish I had kept them! We had so many of them I don't believe we even brought that gallon bucket home.

About the coyotes, one day we saw five coyotes in one pack watching our sheep from a hill about a mile from us. We were too young to carry a gun so all we had was our green willow sticks, which we had learned to use to the best advantage. Well, the coyotes decided not to push their luck that day. The rascals are uncannily shrewd. They would wait till another day to steal a single sheep.

I do remember that the ranch was fenced with a three-strand barbed wire fence, which in later years proved to be quite a chore to ride to and mend. But I always begged Dad to let me go along. It was not long until I was on my own pony and proudly accompanying Dad on his fence inspection trips. During the winter months we always rode with a yellow rain slicker tied on the saddle, because on more than one occasion we had to use them before we returned home. Those cold blue Texas "Northers" sweep right down from

> the Colorado plateau with plenty of sleet and terrifically cold winds. My uncle used to say that there was nothing between the North Plains of Texas and the North Pole except a three-strand barbed wire fence. One day Dad and I were riding out to fix the fence when we came up to where the wind had drifted sand clear up to the top of that barbed wire fence. The cattle had not found it yet, but no doubt would have in time. And how do you fix a fence like that? You just leave the old fence under the sand and build a new one right on top.
>
> And speaking of weather, I well remember our schoolhouse. It was about three miles from us and close to the creek downstream, so when it got cold enough to freeze, the creek was practically solid. What would you expect a bunch of school kids to do given a situation like that? Well, we did a lot of running and skating on the ice, but oh boy, what it did to the soles of our shoes! I remember some good paddlings with Dad's razor strop from the ice skating episodes.

Linda paused again in her reading. Paddlings. She recalled a few of those from her mother who wielded a wooden spoon or a whittled tree branch. But from her father came the dreaded announcement, "I'm going to tan your hide." The memories of her father wielding the razor strop against her bare legs had not departed, though she preferred not to dwell on them. The razor strop had dangled over the bathroom door, a sinister piece of dark leather, its primary use as a sharpening tool for a shaving razor having been transformed into a weapon of control. She had never been a defiant youngster, just curious. Corporal punishment did not begin yesterday. Maybe it started generations earlier. With an inward sigh, she turned once again to the pages.

> My two sisters and brother with our four first cousins from my uncle's family made up eight of the twelve students (some were children of neighboring ranchers or the ranch hands) that my uncle's wife taught at the school, a one-

room unpainted shack. She had experience teaching school back in Texas, so she automatically stood out as the one to teach our country school. She usually rode a trusty mule back and forth the four miles from their home on the west side of the creek so that we kids could get a basic education. Our home was a mile closer to the schoolhouse. It was a small unpainted structure heated in the winter with a pot belly stove burning buffalo chips for firewood. Not just a school teacher, my aunt also filled in as school and community nurse. In addition to taking care of the health of the community, she nursed and fed many a sickly and near frozen lamb from my uncle's flock.

The Palo Duro Creek not only furnished water for the stock and kept the wells fresh with sweet water but offered wonderful fishing, lots of perch and flathead catfish as well as a few yellow channel catfish, which are rarer and quite prized. My mother loved to fish and when she did take us along, that was a real treat for us. Once we had not had much luck during the afternoon, so she decided we should stay at least until dark. We knew the trail back home even in the dark. It was about one mile from the fishing place to our house. We had used grasshoppers and worms and minnows for bait, but the fish just were not biting. Just before dark I baited my hook with a big grasshopper and asked Mother if I could go out about a hundred feet upstream where I often went swimming and knew the water was deeper. She said that we were going home in a few minutes but that I could try the hole. I threw my hook in the water. It was just barely light enough to see my cork, but I saw it go under and I figured a catfish was playing to get my grasshopper, but the line got taut, and I could tell I had something. So I called to Mother and by the time she got there and grabbed the pole I thought I was going to be pulled into the creek. She said we should not jerk or pull too hard, just try to work whatever we had on the hook towards the bank, and some ten minutes later we landed a fish, the likes of which we had never seen pulled out of that creek. To my eight-year-old eyes, it looked like a whale! She helped me lug it home, and it turned out to be a yellow channel catfish over sixteen inches long and weighing over four pounds. You can imagine that after that everyone wanted to fish at that particular spot on the creek. And that is the true fishing story of my life.

Despite all of the challenges, some important memories stay with me. We were two miles from our closest neighbor, twenty miles from the County seat (also our nearest town), thirty-five miles from Guymon, Oklahoma, our nearest railroad town. This isolation from civilization led my mother to try and get a post office at our ranch. Back in those days, it did not take as long to get an answer from Washington as it does today. The Postal Service told her she could have a post office if she was willing to (a) furnish space for the office at no charge and (b) would accept as payment the amount representing stamp cancellations and stamps she sold. She agreed, and as a result she became the official postmistress of Mulock, Texas, Hansford County. Apparently Mulock, Texas, only existed for that period of time and disappeared after we left. How I wish I had kept some letters with that Mulock postmark!

I wrote earlier of the changeable weather prevalent in the Panhandle of Texas. In the winter of 1906-07 it snowed and instead of the usual four inches or so that would be normal, there were several days and nights of it. When it finally stopped we had three feet on level and up to twenty-foot drifts. This meant we could not get feed to any of our stranded cattle some four or five miles from home, so the ranchers knew it was just a question of a few days before those trapped cattle would not make it. The cattle bunched as far they could go over the south fence, then started breaking a trail along the fence row toward the ranch house, and many would have made it down to the creek a short distance from home if it had not been that when they reached the cap rock of the creek canyon they just pushed the front leaders off the forty-foot high rock cliffs into thirty-feet deep snow banks where they just piled on top of each other and simply smothered to death. I remember that on several occasions my brother and I accompanied the ranch hands to where the cattle were stacked. They kept a coal and wood fire going to warm their hands by during the skinning operation. I don't remember how many we lost, but it was the best part of Dad's entire herd.

While the snow was on the ground, lots of jack rabbits hopped in close to our feed lots. We kept several dogs, even some greyhounds to catch coyotes, and the dogs loved jack rabbit meat, so we proceeded to get out in the snow with three-feet long sticks and when we saw a jack rabbit jump out of his hiding place up with his head above the snow, all we had to do was to give the rabbit a good whack on the head and another jack rabbit provided meat for the dogs.

That winter of the big snow was also the coldest of the years we lived in the Panhandle. We saw the creek freeze over solid, at least solid enough that Dad drove across the ice with a wagon loaded with feed for the cattle that had survived. With this below zero weather our dugout became our home. It was completely underground and had one set of stairs to enter and leave by with a fold-over storm door at the top at ground level. That winter we ate and slept in the dugout, with a good supply of dry buffalo chips (probably fifty to one hundred years old). Mother cooked our meals and kept the dugout warm during the daylight hours. Speak of energy conservation! You did not need any fancy insulation to keep a dugout warm in cold weather. Dirt is nature's best insulation, as anyone who has lived in an adobe house will tell you.

The loss of so many cattle coupled with the following two years of drought with blowing sand made Dad decide to quit cattle ranching and go back to farming. He had heard rumors of plenty of irrigation water out in the Salt River Project around Phoenix, Arizona, and also down in the Rio

Grande Valley of Texas. He made a trip to the Rio Grande Valley first and was so impressed he bought forty acres. The land was fertile enough to grow lots of vegetables, so we left the Panhandle in 1909 and relocated just outside a small town of about 3000 souls named San Benito where Mother and Dad set up a dairy farm.

Linda had heard about the dairy farm from her aunt, her father's youngest sister. Missing from her father's writing was an important event – that his father had contracted a serious type of fever and the farm was quarantined. Grandfather's overall health began to deteriorate after that. He was much older than his wife. With no ability to sell milk, and with illness in the family, things became dire. Grandmother decided to set up a boarding house in town, using the services of some of her daughters who still remained at home to do the chores, cooking and upkeep. The family finances took a plunge. Linda pondered about the missing information. Perhaps he knew that his sister was already aware of the circumstances. But Linda suspected something else was going on – a buried shame, having to admit to poverty.

I spent the next ten years there. I graduated from high school in 1916 and entered Rice University at Houston in 1917. My older brother had been attending Texas A&M at College Station, Texas before being drafted into the Army, and he was overseas in Germany at that time. War fever was running so high that over one-half the boys at Rice and other universities were enlisting to beat the draft, so after completing one semester, I decided I would, too. The following July I enlisted in the Naval Hospital Corps, took my boot camp training at New Orleans and was permanently stationed at Pensacola, Florida Naval Hospital for the next fifteen months. Since I was in Reserve status, they kept me on for several months after the Armistice was signed as a technician in the X-Ray room. Working with the X-rays seemed to give me a future that I might like. In fact,

I became obsessed with the idea of getting my college degree and then an MD specializing in radiology or roentgenology, as it was known at the time. I returned to school, but only completed two total years of college at Rice and the University of Texas at Austin.

By this time I knew that I would have to work my way through college and that I could not start earning from my chosen field before I was in my late thirties, so I chucked the MD degree idea and entered the selling business. I did quite well at it but it was not what I had wanted for the lifetime livelihood. The selling field carried me into too much traveling, and I wasn't able to keep a tight schedule on my eating and sleeping habits. I progressed into a victim of allergies and was unable to find a doctor that knew what to tell me to do.

After several months in Brooklyn Naval Hospital in New York, I finally decided I would discipline myself, especially on foods and drink. I began doing this by a very slow process of eliminating the offending foods. It took me several years to establish a pattern that fit my situation. But I had at last found out many of the things I could not eat with the help of a good country doctor who told me in 1928 during another breakdown of my health, "Richardson, what you have with these food allergies will never kill you but they will worry you to death if you let them!"

By 1931, I was in Phoenix, Arizona, after my mother's prayers had delivered me from an unbearable situation. I was a manager in a paint store, and a miracle happened. I met a nurse who had come out west after getting a nursing degree. She was teaching school at the time. So fate intervened and gave me not only a cook and a dietitian, but a wife. I have often wondered how much I have been blessed. At the time of this writing, we have had forty-six years of companionship and LOVE. How fortunate can one human being get?

And that's where the story ended. Linda knew what lay behind the reference to the "unbearable situation." She recalled the time when she was around fourteen, and her mother received a telephone call. Once the receiver was put down, she faced her daughter.

"Well, I suppose you need to know – that was about your father's first wife."

The earth moved beneath her, as if a big sinkhole was opening and she was falling into it. Not to know. Her father, married before, to someone named Sandra. How many other things had been secrets?

"Someone called to say that Sandra passed away."

Linda quizzed her mother for the details and received forthright answers. Her father's earlier marriage had been to a woman who became unfaithful. Not just unfaithful, but a nymphomaniac. They were wed in his early twenties after he had served in the First World War and completed two years of college. He pumped gas at the local filling station, as it was called then. No children had been born as yet, so Sandra worked in a dry goods store selling flirtatious lingerie to the few women in the dirt-poor Texas town who could afford to purchase risqué items, as they were considered in that time, and to women who earned their living in need of such items. One day, he came home early and found Sandra in bed with one of the local policemen.

"He was the last to know," her mother had said. "Everyone else did, even his mother and sisters, also some of their friends. I learned this from his mother, your grandmother. But everyone just felt so sorry for him that no one told him. It was common knowledge that Sandra was sleeping with just about every man in town."

Henry had been devastated, and his health slipped into a steady decline. There was a long period of emotional and physical recovery. He left town but never initiated divorce proceedings. He roamed around to several towns and cities acquiring several different jobs, one of which took him to New York to deliver some packages for his employer. He arrived there on the very day that the banks failed in 1929, and he could not get his paycheck cashed. His body and spirit were so broken that he stayed in the naval hospital for several months, after which a sister sent him money for a bus ticket to Los Angeles. He could stay with her and her husband until he could get on his feet. It was the Richardson way.

"All of this happened before he and I met," her mother continued. "And then, of course, when he proposed to me, he filed for divorce, letting Sandra state before the judge that Henry had deserted her. Linda recalled vividly how her mother had paused, how she had hesitated to speak the next words.

"I know you are troubled by your father's treatment of you. You have asked several times why I didn't leave him. Well, now you know. I couldn't bear to do that after the trauma he had suffered."

❧❦

A cook and a dietitian. Well, Linda could forgive that. Men of her father's generation always looked for a wife to take care of them. But there it was – a professed love for her mother. If she harbored doubts about that devotion, this was proof. She had never heard such sentiments verbalized within the household, but there they were in writing. Did he ever speak the words? She would never know; so much was private between them.

Linda was struck by the capital letters printed by her father in the hand-written memoir. LOVE – he loved her mother deeply. She could not imagine that Larry ever felt that way toward her. That marriage had been over for nearly fifteen years. She had entered it having absorbed the model her father had provided, that the narcissist must be worshipped. With insecurities about herself and wishing to escape the restrictions laid down by her parents, Linda had fled far too early straight into the arms of a man she fell for because she thought he would save her from financial instability.

Larry Frederick Sanders was six years older than she, an Air Force veteran, studying seriously for a business degree, pursuing it with focused energy. With Larry, she would never have to deal with off-beat notions or submit to being humiliated for her reading matter or have her accomplishments ignored, nor would she have to fear sinking into poverty. He was ambitious and wanted to take her along as his helpmate. She allowed herself to be deluded into thinking he was in love with her. The truth was that he turned out to be in love with himself. Was Larry's the same kind of narcissism she detected in her father's collection?

She found her father's writings fascinating for their information but found little expression about his feelings. Chiding herself once more, she searched in vain for some mention of herself, hoping that he would express that she had meant something to him. What had she thought she might find? An early report card marked with A's? School papers with gold stars and "Excellent" written across the top? Some of her early fledgling poetry? Some photos of her? She knew some parents that kept such things.

Linda folded the faded papers. She plucked again at the tufts of the brown chenille bedspread and then dug out threads lodging under her fingernails. Chenille had a long history of being the material of choice for her parents' bed coverings. It was warm in the bedroom, and Linda hoped they could get a decent night's sleep.

Christi entered the bedroom, having finished helping clean up the supper dishes. She curled up on the other twin bed, settling in to continue her 900-page novel about kings and queens of England in the Middle Ages, undoubtedly filled with stories of salacious indiscretions.

"Just a reminder, we're leaving late morning so you can't sleep until noon," Linda said as gently as she could. She knew her daughter's habits. "Wouldn't it make sense to do some packing tonight?" Christi glanced up with a glazed look, giving no indication that she had heard her mother. That was Christi, sailing through life on her own terms.

Just then, Helen Richardson appeared at the door and announced, "You'll be glad to know that I'm turning on the air conditioning."

※※

The next morning, still dazed by the discoveries in the box handed to her by her father, Linda floated toward the bedroom window facing the front yard. The room was still in semi-darkness, so she pulled the cord on the mini-blind, raising the blind fully. Light and warmth streamed into the room. Staring out through the glass to the south, she took in the view of the front yard, a xeriscaped expanse strewn with pebbles where once a green lawn had grown. A variety of ornamental grasses broke up the monotony of the flat gray surface. Some of them had plumes that fanned out at the top like feathers glittering in the morning sunlight. Her eyes roamed around surveying the entirety of the landscape.

"I'm going outside for a few minutes, Christi," Linda said. Christi nodded, then returned to her book. Linda was pleased that her daughter loved to read since reading had brought so much joy into her own life, but she had felt a touch of disappointment when Christi announced at age six that she did not want any more bedtime stories read to her but that she wanted to read her books by herself. From that point, Linda had initiated library trips with Christi, letting her choose what caught her eye, and but also adding some additional volumes to the stacks of books that got carted home to satisfy a curious and determined Christi.

Linda exited the house and strolled leisurely down the front walk. She could tell already that the temperature would rise later to the uncomfortable level of the afternoon before, when she and her father had made their way from the parking lot to the cafeteria.

Suddenly she was filled with the urge to finger the rocks that had replaced the traditional front lawn. She recalled the first house in Albuquerque to which they moved when she was nine. She could still capture the scents in the yard – of lilacs blooming, of roses and bridal wreath – and the feel of sprawling on newly mowed grass, becoming absorbed in a Nancy Drew mystery. But now, water was scarce and yard maintenance time consuming, and many people like her parents had moved to replace their lawns with rocks and desert grasses.

The stones were smoother, rounder than she had realized. Seen from the window, with the sun glinting off them, they had appeared jagged. She bent down, picked one up thinking it might be too hot, but it exuded only faint warmth. Her hand curled around the stone, which pulsed with unexplained energy as she turned it over and over in her palm.

Like beach pebbles without the water, she thought, gathered to decorate front yards in the desert. Examining it closely, she saw that it was not gray as it had first appeared, but a coagulation of pulverized earth rock, no doubt from many geological eras, worn down and crushed and then shaped by cascading mountain waterfalls or crashing ocean waves. Its surface was a composite of infinitesimal pieces ranging from rust to black to copper-colored, a synthesized object appearing one way when viewed from afar, another when studied from a closer angle. Tiny particles coalescing, forming a new substance, each granule with its own history, merging to form the whole.

Linda tossed the pebble away from the house and saw it land near the street near a clump of pampas grass. Suddenly, she caught sight of something tucked under a wide green blade near the bottom. It was brownish with a swooping tail. Jarred into thinking perhaps a cat or a small dog had wandered by, she moved in closer to discover not just one, but a small pair, incongruously placed, of ceramic squirrels.

She turned around, looking toward the house. The spare bedroom faced the street, so that the window with the raised blind caught a reflection of one of the taller stalks of grass. Its image fell against the window, making it appear to be broken, as if something had severed it and let in the outside air. The illusion startled her, perplexed her that she could suspend reality so easily and, if only momentarily, could view this scene from an utterly impossible perspective.

Returning hastily, she found Christi up and dressed and filling her suitcase, at last taking a break from the amours of royalty and the never-ending wars of fourteenth century England. They nodded at each other without exchanging words.

Linda went to the chest of drawers and scooped up her makeup supplies from the maple-colored laminated top, dumping them into a small black vinyl bag and glancing in the mirror above the dresser. Crinkles and fine lines had been forming for some time around her eyes, and there was the start of a droop around her jaw line. From the kitchen, she heard her parents murmuring. Sounds rose and fell signaling a flowing conversation, delivered with a contented mutuality. She could not detect a single sign of the tension so prevalent throughout her childhood.

Morning sunlight poured through the window, but it was not yet as powerful as yesterday afternoon when she and her father had gone to lunch. She slowly lowered the blind, and through the slats, peered out aimlessly at the smooth, sterile stones.

Chapter Four
Many Mansions

In my Father's house are many mansions: if it were not so, I would have told you. I go to prepare a place for you.
— John 14:2

June 13, 1991

Linda drove again to New Mexico at the end of the week for her father's funeral, feeling as if she were wrapped in a time warp. She felt the eeriness of returning so soon and knowing that she would not find her father there. The luncheon trip to the cafeteria and the visit on the patio were a thing of the past, yet only by a few days.

Her sister flew in from California. "I always thought Mother would be the first to go," Shirley said, hugging Linda at the airport in Albuquerque. "You know, all that starving of herself. Do you really think that many foods bother her? What's she going to do now? Who is going to help her out?" Linda cautioned Shirley not to voice those concerns just yet.

"But how is she going to manage – getting groceries and all that?" Shirley persisted. "And what if she gets to the point that she can't even prepare her own meals?"

Linda shrugged and inwardly stifled a wave of panic. As usual, Linda's sister had grasped the full implications of what might lie ahead for their mother while Linda had allowed herself to be lulled into complacency by the cheeriness of her mother's frequent letters. She had never before let herself imagine the "what if's" – a time when her father might no longer be around. Up to now, she had thought it foolish to trouble herself about all contingencies. She was consumed with responsibilities back in Colorado, and her mother's letters always led her to believe that the two of them were able to handle their daily affairs quite handily.

"Daddy and I are doing well, given the various infirmities of our ages," she wrote. "You know how he likes to drive. So don't worry about us."

Her parents had always addressed each other as Mother and Daddy. The incongruity of those expressions had not struck her until she was an adult. Another thing about those letters was that she must have fastened on the *doing well* part and overlooked the word *infirmities*.

Now, facing the loss of her husband, Helen Richardson maintained a stoic appearance in front of her two daughters. Briefly, she summarized what had happened in a straightforward and matter-of-fact way. Her voice crackled, but not because she was about to break down and cry. Just the tightening of the throat that happens with the passing years.

"He hadn't been feeling well and couldn't eat much that evening after you left," she said, referring to Linda's recent visit. "I heard him get up in the night and then heard a plunk. I knew he'd fallen before I reached him sprawled out on the floor. Of course, I called 911, and the paramedics took him to the VA Hospital. They told me that he was dead by the time they arrived. I didn't have them do an autopsy, but it seems that it was the abdominal aneurysm he'd had for a long time."

That was her mother, offering a blunt encapsulation of the end of a remarkable life together. Just eight months ago, they had celebrated their sixtieth wedding anniversary.

Linda tried to express sympathy for her mother's loss. She gave her silent hugs, but words stuck in her throat. She wanted to ask her mother, "How are you going to deal with living alone after all these years of companionship?" But her mother was enveloped in a cocoon of numbness, not ready to deal with such subjects.

"I'd like to get my hair done," her mother announced. Clearly, her focus was on making a good impression at the church service. Linda was relieved that her mother was dealing well with these details. What might lie ahead had to be set aside. Linda called to set an appointment, and the next morning drove her to the salon. The service was scheduled for later that afternoon. Helen Richardson even smiled when examining her hairdo.

"What do you think I should wear?" Usually her mother was more decisive. "I refuse to wear black, and I hope neither of you will do that, either."

Such preoccupations reeked of triviality in the wake of losing a loved one, Linda thought, but she grudgingly realized that these time-honored rituals had a point, to keep going through the motions of life so as to push away the grief engendered by the finality of death.

Linda and Shirley exchanged glances. They nearly interrupted each other in response, but Shirley was the first to answer, "I don't believe in black at funerals either. Besides, it's too hot outside," she added.

Linda's answer was quick, "I wouldn't think of it."

The two sisters were sharing the bedroom with the twin beds. In about half an hour, everyone convened in the living room. Their mother walked steadily out of her bedroom. Unlike so many of her friends of the same age, she did not use a cane. And it was clear that she intended to hold her head high and prove to her church community that she was bearing up well.

"Do you think I look all right? Should I take some breath mints?" Linda wondered why her mother focused on breath mints, of all things, at a time like this. She had chosen a pale blue crepe dress which enhanced her gray curls. Linda and Shirley had bought her a white rose corsage.

Linda looked trim in a tan summer suit while Shirley appeared in a wine-colored peasant blouse and long skirt that flattered her full figure. Linda reassured her mother, "You look fine."

Helen Richardson had not driven for several years. She once wrote to Linda in a letter, "It's my eyes. You know, they never were very good, and now I positively can't see the street signs. But don't be alarmed. Daddy is the greatest driver ever, and he loves to buy the groceries and do all the errands."

Alarm bells should have sounded then, but they did not.

Alighting from the car, Helen reached for each daughter's arm. Three abreast, they strode into the sanctuary. A gathering of about forty friends and well-wishers had already arrived. The minister whisked the three of into a private room behind the front of the church. He exuded kindness and concern.

The building was of 1970s vintage. A gray carpet runner covered the wood floors of the central aisle separating two sets of maple pews. One plain gold cross hung from the ceiling at the front of the church. No pulpit stood on a dais, just three steps up at the front where the preacher delivered his sermon. There were no soaring ceilings or stained glass windows to lift one's spirit to the heavens. A huge pull-down screen was mounted at the front to display the words of the hymns. No hymn books rested in wooden slats behind the backs of each pew. No rounded slots sat ready for communion cups. There was no organ, just a piano.

Tangled wires and microphones had been hastily pushed aside but could not be hidden entirely. No doubt they were meant for a Sunday morning service featuring contemporary Christian rock bands. Linda could not visualize her mother in this type of environment, but there were many things she did not know or understand about her mother.

Somber organ music, piped in via the church's sound system, beckoned people to take their seats, and then all was quiet. Linda and her sister found the front row while the minister escorted their mother to the aisle seat in the same pew. Prayers, hymns and Bible readings followed. To Linda's great relief, her mother had not provided an urn of ashes. Helen Richardson was practical in the face of loss.

Reverend Morrison mounted the steps to deliver the opening words. Holding a Bible, he raised his hand and spoke. His baritone voice was measured, sympathetic, sincere. Those in the pews at first bowed their heads and then raised them to fasten their eyes on the speaker.

"We are all here to mourn the passing of our Brother Henry, whom we all loved so much, and who gave us so much of himself," he began.

Linda's mind suddenly was filled with images of her father. It was as if her brain was lining up a set of photographs taken of him through the years, all plucked from disparate albums that her mother had compiled. Right now, sitting in a church pew, hearing songs and prayers and spoken respects, she wanted more images of him than the recent memory of the diminished man who had turned over a box of his treasures to her. She was tuning out the solemn words of the service, conjuring up a mental construct of what a photo album of his life might look like, if all the scattered snapshots from various albums had been pulled together into a representational collage of his life.

Images floated across her mind's eye. He appeared in black and white glossies with wavy edges, like the one of him as a young boy standing by his horse, or a blurred college photo in one of those full-body swim suits of the 1920s. Or she could see the one of him at age forty-two, debonair with wavy brown hair and a clipped moustache. His brown serge suit held a triangular-folded handkerchief in the pocket. Other pictures flew through her brain, and then one stuck – a snapshot taken of the three of them in the Sandia Mountains when she was a teenager. Her mother wore a turban. Was this the style then? Her father sat on a log, stoop-shouldered with noticeably gray hair. That was over thirty years ago, but Linda had noticed even then how much he had aged.

Suddenly, familiar words brought Linda back to the present. Rev. Morrison was now reading Psalm 90. She exited her visions of photographs of her father and turned her attention to the robed minister. She had heard this psalm recited in her own church with its famous opening lines: "Lord, thou hast been our dwelling place in all generations. Before the mountains were brought forth, or ever thou hadst formed the earth and the world, even from everlasting to everlasting, thou art God."

Dwelling place. Where was her dwelling place? And where, now, for that matter, was her father's? Was it in heaven? The idea of an actual heaven perplexed her. She had released that notion years ago. But clearly, the members of this congregation believed in its existence. Yet, just days ago, while she and Christi headed home, she had dealt with her own confusion when confronted by Christi's question as to whether she believed in heaven. She had not been able to acknowledge Christi's inquiry fully, but she would tell her at some point that she had come to the personal conclusion that it – heaven – could not possibly be like one's earthly living space. But did it resemble something tangible that she could not understand, given her human limitations? Or was it all an illusion, a construct of the human brain?

And then, as if in gentle rebuttal, as if her mind had been an open book, Rev. Morrison segued to a passage from the New Testament.

"The Bible tells us in John 14:2, 'In my Father's house are many mansions: if it were not so, I would have told you. I go to prepare a place for you.' This means that once we pass on, true believers in Christ will be resurrected to be with God and Christ in heaven. I have no doubt that Brother Henry is now up there among the saints, and is experiencing much joy."

With those words, a subdued murmur of assent rose from the congregation. To Linda's astonishment, hands began waving and voices began chanting over and over, "Praise

Brother Henry! Praise Brother Henry! Praise our Brother!" Soon the congregation was on its feet, swaying as the pianist blasted out "When the Saints Go Marching In."

Her father had worn many masks: mining prospector, community and church leader, salesman, sympathetic protector of those less fortunate, creative ne'er-do-well, inventor, card reading devotee, UFO believer, benign neglecter. Now he was being elevated by implication to the status of sainthood. Was her father a saint? What makes a saint?

As the raucous response slowly diminished, Linda sent a knowing glance at her sister, as if trying to communicate an invisible shrug. Neither had attended a memorial service like this. Nothing like it had ever happened during the years of their sedate Presbyterian upbringing. Linda noticed that during the "praise" expressions, her mother had sat quietly, her eyes focused on the front of the church. Those eyes betrayed no emotion. Her mother was adept at hiding whatever roiled inside.

After the service, those attending were invited to a reception provided by church members in the commons area. Plates of sandwiches, cheeses, fruit, nuts and cookies sat on long tables all provided to celebrate her father's life. Throughout generations and different cultures, the community rallied to soothe the grief-stricken, the caregivers, the survivors. And food was always a part of it all. Food from friends, food from strangers. Food, the bread of life, followed when a neighbor or friend learned about a failure of the body to thrive, or in its finality, a failure to survive.

Although she felt that she was stuck in a foreign country, Linda could not help but be moved by the generosity of her parents' church community. Their concern, their care, their willingness to come and pay respects and be supportive to her mother – all these wiped away any theological differences or those of worship style.

Linda's mother bore up well, smiling even, as she took in the many expressions both of sympathy for the loss of her husband, and of joy for his long life. He had been admired for his speaking skills and for his leadership on several church committees. Linda took this in but continued to struggle with her own view of her father, which never matched that of the outside world.

Shirley chatted away with people she had never met as if they were long lost friends. Linda admired Shirley's outgoing personality; in fact, she was a bit envious. Shirley had always been that way, gregarious and friendly. Dark curls bobbed around her smiling face, and from her throat came a hearty laugh. She possessed the kind of natural self-confidence that Linda had to work to attain. She wondered whether some people were born with a sense of self, while others had to acquire it slowly over many years.

After smiling and nodding her way along with the line of people filling their plates, Linda withdrew to a quiet corner of the room to recoup her energy. Alone now, she puzzled over how her mother's quiet and diffident personality fit in with this church. She had asked about that at one time, maybe too bluntly, but her mother explained that while she did not relate to the style of the services, the pastor was so brimming with God's love, and the people so supportive, that she went along with her husband's choice.

Many mansions. Linda wondered whether her mother believed, as the preacher had intoned, that the spouse she had just lost was literally, physically taken up into one of those mansions to be in heaven with the angels and the saints and Jesus and God.

In a conversation at one time, Linda had probed for more clarification from her mother about her views on this subject. Her answer was neither defensive nor ingratiating. Nor was it obscure, but as always, straight to the point.

"I don't have to agree with every single thing they do or believe. They don't ask me or require me to pledge to anything, just to belong. I have found a God of love instead of the frightening God of my childhood. And a community that cares. That's enough for me. I have found peace."

Linda was now unraveling part of the mystery of her mother – her pattern of quiet accommodation to those things which she believed that she could not change.

※

The memorial service had triggered recollections of days past, emotional responses that Linda thought she had long put away. On the way home, her mind wandered, thinking about those early years when they lived in anything but real-life earthly mansions. The root meaning of "mansions," she knew, meant "rooms." In some Bible translations, this is the word used. The rooms of Linda's childhood were few, but the houses were many.

Before she was old enough to recall events of those very early years of life in a city at the edge of the Sonoran desert, Linda relied on her mother's stories of the beginnings of a journey that would send the family down a precarious path. Their lives were uprooted not once but many times. They were destined to live in many homes.

During Linda's infancy and first two years, the family had lived in a small but tidy stone house. In the neighborhood, there were other young parents with laughing, happy children.

"I was so contented then," Linda's mother said, blinking her hazel eyes. "It was the life I dreamed of, until I lost that baby. But then to have you – it was all I ever wanted. Life was good. There were several babies in our neighborhood born around the same time, so you had plenty of friends from an early age. I watched all of you carefully in the sandbox because where we lived, there were scorpions."

As it turned out, real scorpions were not the problem, but rather the sting of a coming disruption to the family. Linda's father was becoming restless with his work as a sales manager for a paint company. He disliked the travel; however, it was a secure position, sound enough that Linda's mother need not work outside the home.

Then one day, when Linda was almost three, her father returned home from work and told her mother announced excitedly, "See, I have this offer from Don Hightower – you remember him – and it's such a good opportunity, I plan to take it. It will be a huge jump in salary. And if I do well, I can become a partner in the firm."

Almost as an afterthought, he added, "It's in Albuquerque, so we will be moving east. The climate is supposed to be much better there."

Her father could not resist the possibility of easy money, and this friend apparently was getting very rich quickly. He did not ask her mother whether this turn of events suited her. Of course, she would go; she was obligated to follow her husband. It was not destiny, but duty. Her parents rented a house one block off Central Avenue, the famous Route 66. She could still picture the hardwood floors, spacious backyard and screened-in front porch, which became a playroom.

Once again, there were neighborhood children to play with. Among other things, they enjoyed pushing miniature doll buggies down the sidewalks near their houses. One day, after playing outside with a friend in the morning, Linda came home for lunch but left the buggy parked outside the front door. Money was scarce in those days, and so were toys. Upon returning outside, Linda discovered that the doll carriage had vanished. Linda's mother went from house to house seeking her daughter's possessions, to no avail. But a few days later, Linda saw from the picture window an older child from an adjacent block sauntering by with Linda's toy doll stroller; if not that, at least an exact replica. They knew who the child was and where she lived, though she was not one of Linda's playmates.

Her mother rushed outside and caught up with the supposed thief. But before she could utter an accusatory word, the child smirked, shook her head, and sprinted off, thrusting the doll carriage in front of her and disappearing around the corner at the end of the block. Linda had never seen her mother so furious. By now Linda was outside, too, clutching her mother's apron as together they hurried over to the next street where the buggy pusher lived. The rap on the door should have alerted someone, but no one came to answer.

As they walked home empty handed, her mother dished out retribution. "Next time, don't leave your things out. It's your fault." Those words, "It's your fault," were to be spoken over and over again in the next few years.

Linda's father decided to paint the gray concrete floor of their front porch brick red. He showed Linda how to hold a paint brush and let her dip it in the can of paint, which smelled of old socks dipped in turpentine. She took pride in being of help to her father, and she swashed the brush onto the floor of the porch with gleeful abandon.

That night she dreamed that she had painted herself into the corner of the porch and, to get outside, she had to set her shoes down on the wet red paint. Then somehow, she was inside a doll buggy turned red instead of gray canvas cloth. It raced along the street on its own power as if propelled by a ghost. The dream ghost pursued her shouting, "It's your fault, it's your fault."

That was the beginning of a long parade of reproaches for not measuring up to her parents' expectations. Too often her head was in the clouds, dreaming of beautiful sky colors, of a world where she could play all day and come home happy. Sometimes when she forgot her things, even the disapproval that awaited was not enough to shake her childhood reveries.

Despite the debacle with the lost doll carriage, life settled into a regular routine. But trouble was brewing, and larger concerns loomed in her parents' lives. The Asian front of the Second World War was on, and rubber was rationed because the Japanese had invaded what was then called the Dutch East Indies and claimed its rubber plantations. With rubber now in short supply and needed for military artillery, the United States government set up a system of rationing scarce goods. Automobile tires were among the first items to be put on the ration list. To get a new tire, a car owner had to certify to a local board that no more than five tires were owned.

Through a massive advertising campaign, the government urged people to turn in scrap rubber, for which they would be paid a penny per pound. Linda's father's acquaintance had created a business of soliciting discarded rubber items and paying the donors a half a penny per pound, to save them the bother of having to take their scrap to the collection centers. Once a large enough load had been collected, it would be hauled off and the government's remuneration pocketed. It was a door-to-door effort. Henry Richardson's success as a paint salesman qualified him to be the perfect persuader.

What her father did not know but discovered eighteen months later was that his "friend" had been profiteering on the black market by legitimately purchasing tires with ration stamps, and then turning around and re-selling them for higher than normal prices to the well-heeled who had exhausted their ration stamps. The scrap rubber collection was merely a front for a more nefarious undertaking. Since tires were rationed, those who could afford to and who were willing to risk buying on the black market could replace their worn-out tires more frequently. Of course, they turned a blind eye as to how the new tires were acquired. They only knew they had a source.

Only when her father was asked to abandon collecting rubber scraps and start re-selling tires did he finally tumble to the shady business into which he had been duped.

Such activities were punishable by prison terms. Horrified at the criminality and frightened of the consequences, he demanded to be bought out from his share of the partnership. Don Hightower, while believing that the secret would not be revealed because of Henry's own complicity, nevertheless did pay up.

Linda's mother tried to persuade her husband to invest the sizeable buyout sum in land in Albuquerque and to train to be a real estate salesman. With his talent, she had no doubt that he would do well and that such a path would offer security for the family. However, Henry Perchfield Richardson had other ideas.

He embraced the turn of events with naïve optimism. Never fear; all would be well. He would dig for minerals, and they would know riches beyond what they could imagine. Waving away any pronounced displeasure from her mother, Linda's father stayed firm. This was his chance, and he was not going to lose it.

The money from the erstwhile partner running the spurious venture had been her mother's hope for a down payment on a new home, and startup cash needed for a new business, but the precious sum got squandered. The oozing away of the nest egg began with a parade of trips to the state capital to obtain mining permits that pointed out unpopulated regions where maps indicated there could be lucrative "digs."

Thus it came to be that Linda's father took the family south, driving slowly through the Isleta Pueblo Indian village, then through farmland planted with beans, squash and corn, and finally to a town where rows of cottonwoods flanked the sides of irrigation ditches paralleling the Rio Grande River. He chose this place because it was known as the Railroad Center of New Mexico. Being here would put him closer to the possible mining spots he planned to claim, and it was essential to be near a railroad.

Once he struck gold or silver, or mined for copper, he envisioned acquiring huge contracts for the ore. He used some of the money to purchase digging equipment. He also rented a warehouse fifty miles away from the three-room adobe house in which he had installed his wife and daughter. Then he proceeded to leave for days on end, camping out in the warehouse, stashing his equipment there, spending his days prospecting.

During the times he stayed at home, Henry Richardson became active in the small but thriving community, joining a church and civic organizations. In these groups, he made friends with like-minded men who shared his vision of striking it rich. Dismayed and disheartened, Linda's mother protested at the folly of his quixotic adventures, but to no avail.

"He got this trait from his father and uncles down in Texas. They were always moving from one get-rich-quick venture to another. A herd of cattle here, a farm there, but none of them ever panned out," she told Linda. "Just too bad they never bought land on which they might have struck oil.

"At least they were honest Presbyterians," she continued. "They tried everything but cattle rustling. But all of their efforts failed, some because of bad luck, some because of not checking out the facts closely enough. I remember visiting his family in Texas. All they could do was sit around talking about the glories of the Richardson men while their wives and daughters worked themselves to death waiting on them and keeping the family together. And as for that business venture, your Dad's 'friend'..."

Her mother paused as if trying to gather just the right words to describe her frustration. "I fault myself for not urging your father to check out the details more closely. Seems it takes a salesman to fall for a salesman. And then, there were those fortune tellers..."

Henry Perchfield Richardson sought out clairvoyants in times of crisis in his life when the choices before him seemed too murky, too unsettled to determine what path to take. Just months before he met Helen Catherine O'Brien, the psychic he was seeing predicted that soon he would meet an exceptional woman, and that she would consent to marry him.

"She'll be a queen," was her definitive word.

The psychic also told him that he would indeed become rich through mining the earth. As she studied his palm, she scooped up the coins he presented. Facing him solemnly, in a ghost-like whisper, she intoned, "You will find your fortune out of the ground."

※

Linda had been resting in an easy chair with her eyes closed, allowing her mind to sift through the many memories that had brought her to this day. Shirley was at the kitchen table sorting through pictures, offering to take them home with her and assemble them in an album.

"I'm getting tired, girls," their mother said. "It's been a long day, but I'm glad you were with me today at the service." Linda and Shirley looked at one another. Helen O'Brien Richardson was not inclined to hand out compliments.

"Of course," Linda said hastily. "Is there anything we can do to help before we all get ready for bed?"

"Well, you might go out and see if that shed in the back yard is locked up tight. You know your father was afraid that it would get vandalized, and all the castor oil is there plus his contraption to distill water."

Another exchange of suppressed amusement shot between the two sisters. It was as if after all these years of not communicating and leading vastly different lives, they bonded in a solemn pact, remembering their father's peculiar habits and their mother's indulgence of them.

Before drifting off to sleep, Linda's thoughts returned to the successive "many mansions" of her childhood, thoughts triggered by the message in the Biblical passage.

After moving away from Albuquerque, the first house they lived in was a tiny adobe. The floor had rough-sawn boards that needed to be covered with rugs to avoid getting splinters. Outside, Linda dragged her hands along those unplastered bricks stuck with straw. It felt like rubbing a stiff hairbrush across her palms. The house sat among towering cottonwoods near a huge drainage ditch. Her father constructed a swing, sanding smooth a tiny seat and boring holes for the ropes, which, knotted tight, got looped and tied around low branches. An unpaved road ran several yards away from this dirt play yard, but she was instructed to stay close – the ditch and the road were off limits.

Within a year, however, her father became restless again and decided to move his family closer into town. No more rough mud walls – this was a step up, he announced. Her mother became more cheerful, for now they were close to their church, downtown for shopping, and the movie theater.

Vaguely, Linda could remember leaving her beloved swing behind, but that now there would be a fenced backyard where she could play on a lawn instead of in the dirt. She remembered hearing her mother tell her that the town council planned to install swings and a slide in a nearby park. There was a real sidewalk leading from the front porch flanked by planter beds where Linda's mother could tend roses. Best of all, Linda was presented with her first pet, an adorable gray kitten.

Up the street on the next block lived some children slightly older than Linda. Sociable, desirous of playmates, she ventured into the front yard, then down the sidewalk. Three girls, one Linda's size and two older ones, maybe by a couple of years, approached her. Their brown skin shone in the relentless sun. Their cotton dresses were tied in back with bows, and all of them had dark hair that hung straight or curled around their faces. Linda pulled down shyly on the canvas hat that shaded her eyes and held her auburn pigtails in place.

"Hi, I'm Linda," she said, in a tentative five-year-old voice. She tugged on her pinafore, not knowing what she should do to claim their attention.

They stood there, gawking at her. Then they looked at each other, covering their mouths and giggling. Together, they turned around and started to run away. Linda was perplexed. As she stood there wondering what to do next, the tallest girl turned and shouted, "We'll be back, we want to get something for you!"

Linda turned away – she had ventured past only a couple of houses – feeling discouraged. These girls probably would not become playmates. Just as she took the first step up to her front porch, she saw the three girls rushing toward her.

"Come on, come down to the sidewalk," the smallest one called. Linda turned and complied with the request.

"We brought you something," one of them said. Tentatively, Linda retraced her steps, approaching them cautiously.

"Hold out your hand. It's candy."

Willingly, Linda stretched out her right hand, palm facing up. Candy was not readily available because of sugar rationing, so someone must have made this from left-over allotments. Sweets were not permitted in Linda's household, and she knew she would have to throw it away, but she wanted to please these new friends who were offering her a treat.

Then the pain pierced her palm and she screamed. Down came some kind of device stuck with pins or nails or blades. Drops of blood oozed from where each prick had entered the skin.

The three brown girls pulled away, turned again and ran once more down the street, crying, "Anglo! Anglo! Gringa!"

When Linda stumbled into her living room, sobbing, her mother's arms embraced her.

This was also the place where she had learned that her parents were not always truthful with her. She noticed her father's sly wink at her mother when he said, "Looks like your kitty ran away. Now don't cry!" Her father could never abide tears. Even when he applied the razor strop, he admonished her, "Hush! Hush!" Years later, Linda's mother did confess the truth. After failing to use its litter box and despoiling the new bedspread in her parents' room, the kitten had been delivered to the country and let out of the car to fend for itself.

"We had no choice, you see," her mother told her. In later years, Linda wondered if she meant the abandonment of the kitten or the speaking of the lie.

Chapter Five
An Ordinary Day

July 16, 1945

Rising just before dawn as she always did, Helen Richardson yawned and turned down the sheet, careful not to disturb her sleeping husband. Shafts of daylight crept under the pull-down shade covering the bedroom window, falling in a slanted line across the linoleum covered floor. Dust motes wafted lazily above the bed, tiny reminders of the cottony strands of fluff floating lazily outside from the ubiquitous cottonwood trees. The air in June had been filled with them, but on this July morning only a few remained, as if suspended in time. The uncomfortable warmth of last night had made it difficult to sleep, but as always, the temperature dipped toward morning, allowing for a few hours of precious slumber.

Although she was not pleased about having to move from the house near the church, Helen found something each day worthy of gratitude. She did not complain about the heat, even in the height of a blistering southwestern summer. The air was dry and crisp, sometimes too dry, and everyone wished for rain.

In her earlier life growing up in the Midwest she would more than once awaken to a dreary sky heavy with humidity. She knew when the sun was rising over the ridge trying to penetrate the gray mist. She could see filtered light through the haze from the upstairs window of the farmhouse, but usually the sun itself could barely be discerned. Those were days when she and her sisters felt bathed in a thin soup ladled from a cauldron.

As she slid carefully out of bed, the coiled bedsprings squeaked, and her husband stirred but did not awaken. She scratched her nose and raised her fingers to her head to pull off the hairnet and laid it on her dresser. She had few luxuries but insisted on protecting the waves in her short-bobbed hair, now sprouting a few silver strands at the temples. Sliding her feet into a pair of scuffed pink slippers, she wrapped herself in a blue chenille robe to cover her thin nightgown and padded out to the front door to pick up the milk.

Today was Monday. Yesterday the family had gone to church as was their custom, and afterwards she had served a variation of the traditional Sunday meal, an extravagance, given their financial circumstances. This time, instead of fried chicken, she had simmered a venison pot roast with carrots, onions and potatoes. Canned green beans and slices of freshly baked bread slathered with butter had rounded out the meal.

This morning was the start of a new, ordinary week. Her husband Henry was stirring but not yet fully awake, and their five-year-old daughter Linda was sleeping peacefully in the second bedroom. Helen hid her fears that Linda would have trouble adjusting to the third house in two years, especially since she was now bereft of her kitten. The hope for stability, for security, was fading fast.

On her way through the kitchen, she glanced at the clock – 5:25 a.m. The milk would have been delivered by 5, so she must get it into the icebox. The iceman had delivered a chunk yesterday, so the milk would stay cold for a few days. The ice ruled the timing of their menus. Just yesterday, her husband had tied up a chicken by its legs to the clothesline outside and whacked off its head with an ax. Blood sputtered all over the dirt yard. Then he swiped the rope with the ax, releasing the headless creature to tear around the yard until it finally collapsed into a limp russet and brown heap.

Helen wondered whether she should have allowed Linda to watch the whole scene from behind the kitchen screen door. Henry gutted the chicken outside, saving the giblets, then carried the deceased hen into the kitchen. Working deftly on the wooden countertop that adjoined the sink, Helen dumped the giblets into a pan to boil up for soup stock, then plucked feathers, turning the poor fowl into a wrinkled tan blob with two stick-like legs. Later she would grind the cooked liver and heart and mix it up with mayonnaise for sandwich spread and shred out every last morsel from the back to add to the soup. She then expertly sliced up the legs, thighs and breast, wrapped them in wax paper and stowed them in the ice box.

"I used to do this all the time when I was growing up," she said to Linda, who stared at the whole process in wide-eyed wonder. "No one else wanted to learn, so I did. It's messy, yes, but has to be done."

Outside, the air was cool, and she could hear a mourning dove in the distance. Helen enjoyed these early summer mornings before the other two household inhabitants awakened. Robins chirped, elm leaves rustled, and a breeze lifted the yellowed and curling window shade. She caught the smell of hay growing in a field at the end of the block, just down the road. It reminded her of growing up on a farm hundreds of miles from where she lived now.

She now looked to the east toward the towering mountains where an edge of lemon-colored light crept upwards. Dawns began with a deep blue sky fading to turquoise when punctured by a rising sun. The mountains emerged slowly from a somber sky, first dove gray, followed by soft blue with craggy streaks as the sun rose behind them. She stopped to take in a deep breath, silently thanking the good Lord for the earth-scented air, for the sun clearing the sky of inky streaks, for robins and roadrunners and for all of the beauty and, yes, even drudgery that lay ahead in yet another commonplace day.

Just as Helen leaned down to pick up the bottle of milk, suddenly, the neighborhood dogs began to yowl – what's this? They never had created such a disturbance. Then, a faraway muffled boom and a blinding flash. It came in the southern sky which was still dark but mottled with patches of daylight. She instantly lifted her arm to cover her eyes. Peeking carefully from behind her hands, she saw that now the image was fading into a peculiar shape at the top, billowing out like the head of a toadstool.

Rattled, puzzled, she returned to the bedroom and found that her husband was already up and dressed. She wondered if the sound, although muted, had awakened the others. She hurriedly put on a muslin housedress and rolled up cotton stockings to just above her knee where she secured them with garters. Finishing up, she pulled on and laced up her low-heeled brown oxfords. She took the few steps to the kitchen where she began fixing breakfast – oatmeal garnished with fresh berries grown and generously furnished by the neighbors, one piece of bacon for each and buttered toast. Coffee for herself and her husband, a glass of milk for Linda.

The smell of the bacon, the scent of coffee – these were the mainstays of her very ordinary life. Helen reminded herself not to take such simple pleasures for granted, even if Henry did, and Linda was too young to grasp the passing of time and the knowledge that somewhere, someday, these mornings would be different. How different might not be known, but they would be different. She was sure of that.

"You can't believe how it lit up the sky," she said to her husband, who began pouring a generous amount of cream on his cereal.

"Well, I expect we'll hear about that soon," he said, slurping his coffee.

"Mother, what was it?" asked Linda.

"Hard to say, dear, but you know there's a war going on overseas. There are lots of bombs being used over there. Maybe they were testing something."

"Will the bombs hit us?" Linda asked.

"Our country is safe," her mother answered assuredly. But she sighed, hoping that she had not misled her daughter.

When Helen was a young teenager, out in the fields, calling the cows home, her brother rushed up to her shouting excitedly, "There's war in Europe! I wish I was eighteen – I'd enlist!" That's the closest the war ever came to her life. It was always something "over there," something to read about in the newspapers, like the sinking of the Titanic a few years earlier.

"I'm going to be gone a few days," Henry said, rapidly changing the subject and interrupting his wife's thoughts about wars past.

Helen stifled a look of disapproval. But she quickly submerged it, thinking that if it had not been for his age, he might be away at war, certainly longer than a few days. And he might never have come back. She had comforted more than one friend who had become a widow. Her husband was almost forty-two when Linda was born, two months after Hitler invaded Poland.

The three of them were seated around the green Formica table with a metallic rim. Green was Helen's favorite color, and when a fellow church member mentioned that he was selling the set, she begged Henry to buy it. The chairs, like the table itself had curved chrome tubular legs. One of the foam seats had a slight tear and some tufts of stuffing were threatening to protrude.

Henry was always changing the subject, never wanting to talk about what was happening in the world unless those events affected him directly, or if he could pontificate on their meaning as if he had some inside information.

This war is the same as the last one, Helen thought, a remote happening that does not interfere with our daily lives. The ice man comes tomorrow. The milk will arrive as always. The mourning dove will coo, and Linda and I will eat our oatmeal alone. Dust will be everywhere inside and out, but the sunflowers will shimmer with golden petals, and the mountains will turn pink in the evening. At night, I will read to her from the *Old Testament Bible Stories* and recite poetry to her. Yes, it was going to be just another nothing-out-of-the-ordinary day.

※

Henry Richardson, too, was gearing up for his run-of-the-mill day. He would go down to his business establishment for a while. But he'd be off later in the afternoon for places down south where he planned to stake a mining claim, isolated places in the desert with only sagebrush and rabbits to remind a human intruder that any kind of life could flourish there.

"That trip to Santa Fe was worth it," he announced. "I got the claim I wanted. It's a mineral no one has heard of, but it's going to make us rich."

Always trying to take an interest in her husband's outside activities, yet hating them, too, she said, "And what might that be?" She meant, what mineral.

Getting rich was not what she wanted out of life, rather to have her husband pay attention to his business and to support the family. She had been to the edge too many times, not knowing where their next meal might be coming from. She wanted more opportunities for Linda, maybe even a town or city with a larger library. Still, she was grateful that the Woman's Club in the town had put together a small lending library. She had made good use of it. And she had managed to squirrel away enough pennies to start a small shelf of permanent volumes – poetry like *A Child's Garden of Verses*, and popular books like *Winnie the Pooh*, *Mary Poppins* and *Just So Stories*. Years later she would smile when Disney popularized many of the stories she had enjoyed sharing with Linda, who devoured them on her own once she had learned to read.

"Trust me," he would say to Helen, when he caught the edge in her voice signaling her disapproval. "You're going to have a much nicer house than this one some day."

Is that what he yearned for? A better house? Or simply the ability to brag to his friends about his success? She wondered what her husband would do with lots of money, whether the change in circumstances would come, ironically, with unwanted excesses. She asked herself whether the riches he sought would make the two of them and Linda any happier. Perhaps they *would* buy a handsome home with hardwood floors and furnish it with plush carpets and oak antiques as they'd seen in the homes of their more prosperous friends.

But would there be a cost to climbing up in the world and being acknowledged by the top rung of town leaders? Henry was already getting acquainted in his work in several community organizations, but he had expressed that sometimes he had not broken into their inner circle. Helen knew why. She too had wished for more socializing with some of these people. They had received a few invitations, but she had dodged reciprocating out of embarrassment about their run-down dwelling and meager furnishings.

Of course, she would never decline an improved housing situation, but other desires took priority, like maybe taking a vacation. The local paper was full of paragraphs about visits and trips taken by Henry's friends. In earlier days, when they lived in Arizona, they had escaped the unbearable summer heat by going to the West Coast where they enjoyed the beaches and the cool ocean breezes. That was when Henry had steady, predictable employment, and they could afford to get away occasionally. They had even taken Linda to the beach before she was a year old, to dig in the sand and splash in the waves. There were photos of her holding Linda at the shoreline of the Pacific Ocean. Those days were gone.

Helen worried a great deal about Linda's future. She had high hopes that her daughter would be able to go to college, if only…but Henry Richardson had squandered their nest egg before, so what might he do if he truly got his hands on some money? Gamble it away on yet another hopeless pursuit? At some point, they would no longer be able to work and needed to save some money for their old age. Was she the only one who thought ahead? But he got ruffled when she mentioned these things. "If you've got money, I say, spend it," was his motto.

Henry's voice pierced through her thoughts. "Ricolite. I'll bet you never heard of it. It's found only in the southwestern part of the state. It's a green stone. Has cream and black stripes, beautiful, and now it's being made into all kinds of things for sale – jewelry, bookends, ash trays, things like that. I think we'll have a corner on the market," he spoke excitedly.

Helen Richardson knew that "we" meant his partners. Some were from church, others from his Rotary Club. A prominent banker and oddly enough, the minister of their church, too, had all gone in on the project. She figured that all of them were either fools or adventurers. It disturbed her that every one of them except her husband had enough resources to fall back on should the venture fail.

Helen sighed. It was mostly an inward and controlled movement of breath away from her lips, nothing that anyone, surely not Henry Perchfield Richardson, would notice.

How much longer could Henry sustain his business? Helen was troubled because she kept the books and knew things were going south for the photography studio. He was beginning to re-schedule appointments in favor of his out-of-town trips, and customers who had hoped for wedding pictures at a certain time were not pleased. Just recently, another photographer had moved into town. Helen knew what that meant – competition. It was inevitable that Henry would not remain forever unchallenged.

He had charmed the bank president, Joseph Catron, into yet another loan to keep things running. Now, because of his running off to the desert so much, he had to hire an assistant to manage the business while he was away. So another $3,000 had suddenly appeared. That's when Henry perked up. That amount of money would keep them afloat for maybe another year. Helen suspected that Mr. Catron possibly was a silent partner in the ricolite venture. He never had asked to examine the accounts nor required the submission of a business plan. She wondered if all bankers were so casual. Henry simply scoffed at those details.

"It's who you know, and how much they trust you," he would say when she brought up the subject.

Helen knew the numbers, for she meticulously entered sales and expenditures in the ledger. She did not believe in debt, or very little, only when there was a high probability of a flow of funds coming in from customers, enough to retire the startup loans and to provide sustenance for the family. But Henry was not servicing properly the customers who ultimately put food on their table.

However, whenever she tried to bring up the subject, Henry brushed her aside. "Have some faith in me," he said. "Everything's going to turn out well, and you will become a rich woman." There it was again – his goal, not hers.

"We can start by selling the ore to the Zuni Indians. They're the ones that live west of here near Arizona. They polish it up and make jewelry and fetishes."

"What's a fetish, Daddy?"

※

Linda's curiosity was forever getting her into trouble, especially in church. Outside, she delighted in running up and down the church steps. During the service, she whispered.

"What's the lamb of God, Mother? I don't want to be washed in the blood of the lamb! Why does Jesus love me? What is the valley of the shadow? I saw my shadow when I walked home, but it wasn't in a valley." On and on, until

Helen would poke her in the arm and run a finger across her mouth.

For her daughter's behavior, Helen paid the price. She was shunned by the friendship circle of church women. They talked behind her back, clucking that she could not or would not control her daughter. A church friend, perhaps with a guilty conscience, alerted her to the reason. At some point, she would tell Linda how she felt about being excluded during those years, how it reminded her of her own father's treatment of her as she grew up. *Friendship*, she would say, with a trace of bitterness in her voice, recognizing that despite her best efforts to forgive, she had not managed to be entirely successful. "I always thought that group was so misnamed."

❧❦

"A fetish, well, it's a – oh, I think some kind of object like an animal and they think it has magical powers." Her father stumbled a bit trying to come up with a plausible answer. "The Indians think it might be a spirit."

"Well, does it? Is it magic? Was the bright light that Mother saw a spirit?"

"No more questions, Daughter. I have to be off," he said. And he looked at his wife and delivered his famous wink accompanied by a sly grin. Helen managed a wry smile. Someday, when Linda was older, she would tell her about that other definition of "fetish," the one with the salacious meaning. Perhaps, then, Linda could find that amusing, too.

"But what if that explosion – it was so dazzling – means there is danger down south," Helen looked with pleading hazel eyes at her husband.

"You're always worrying too much," he scoffed. "Whatever it was is over, and we'll hear soon enough. I'm not going get upset over things I can't control."

"So you'll be gone, I guess," she said, expressionless. "I had planned on having a fried chicken dinner tonight."

"Just for a few days. That's all." Henry arose from his chair and walked to the bedroom to pack a small bag for his trip.

⁓✥⁓

That night, Helen dreamed that she and a little girl who looked like her young daughter, but not exactly, lay down on some railroad tracks with their heads on pillows. "We're coming here so that we can be safe from the bombs," the woman in the dream said.

"Are we safe from the war bombs, Mommy?" the little girl asked her mother.

"Of course, I told you, the war is over there. We're here where it's safe."

No trains appeared in the dream.

Trains and railroads haunted Helen. Here she was living in a town whose major economic support was the railroad. But there had been other trains in her past. A train missed in her girlhood reminded her of unpleasant memories of her difficult relationship with her father.

Once when Helen was seventeen and helping take care of the family, she watched her father standing by his desk. It was stacked with papers. Her father had called her to come to him; he had something to say to her. Her hazel eyes widened, flickering with a glimmer of hope that he would talk to her. But he turned away and stared at the wedding photograph hanging on the wall above the desk. He was preparing to abandon the farm and move all of them, her five sisters and one brother, to town. He could not bear staying in the same place where his wife had taken her own life.

"Drank lye, she did," whispered their Irish neighbors, "you know, from makin' the soap. So sad – she just got worn down."

"We'll pack the furniture onto the train," he said, still not looking at her, and twirling his moustache. Oh, thought Helen, so that's it. He wants to tell me when we'll get started. She assumed that she would get to help lift and load. There was not much furniture, only beds and a few dishes and cookware. She always wanted to do what the others did, but somehow she never felt that she quite fit. Her head, as she later put it, was always in the clouds, always thinking about religion, a magnetic force in her life that both attracted and repelled her. But now was a chance to prove herself useful and a genuine part of the family.

"You're going with me ahead of time," her father announced. "I need you to help out to cover the cost of my room and board in this boarding house while I get everyone else settled. I worked it out with the landlady. You'll be fixing meals, cleaning, cooking…things like that."

Helen was stunned. "But – but – don't I get to help load our goods and then ride the train with everyone?"

"But-but," he echoed her voice, pitching his guttural vocal chords as high as they would reach. Waves of shame engulfed her. He had done this to her before too many times, mimicked her voice in front of the others. What was wrong with her? Why wasn't she liked by him? He respected her older sisters and held a protective fondness for two younger ones. Not surprisingly, he favored his only son above all others. Somehow, she had got wedged in the middle of the brood, and he always acted as if he resented her presence. What had she done to displease him? Looking back on those days, she wondered if he saw her as too much like his wife, her mother. Too diffident, too cowed by his strong personality ever to speak up in her own self-defense.

Now she retreated to the farm yard, stalked out to the henhouse, caught a chicken, took up the ax and chopped off its head. She carried it down to the spring where she washed off the blood from her hands. She daubed at spots on her clothes and then dunked the bird several times. She bent far over the water, holding the chicken by its feet to shake off the last drop, trying to avoid spattering her clothes. Then she headed back to the farmhouse where she plucked out the feathers, cut it up into pieces, and stewed it that night for the family dinner. She prepared the entire meal, serving the hen with boiled potatoes, sliced tomatoes from the garden, and slabs of buttered bread which she had rolled out, kneaded and baked that morning.

After the move was complete, Helen stoically endured the report of her shiny-eyed sisters who had returned from the train trip and helped unload the furniture and scanty belongings into the house their father had rented. Why was she always left out? She was good at household tasks. Was that why her father elected her to exchange her services for his room and board? But did he have the right? She was nearly an adult woman and was being treated as a child. It was not an option in her household to defy the father.

Helen's answer to all her childhood loneliness was to escape. She stayed home after high school and teachers' college for a while. Then, in her mid-twenties, she gathered up a few clothes and her self-regard and left the family, the only one to do so, to enter nursing school. But one thing she vowed was that if she ever married, it would be to someone who valued her, someone who did not make her feel unworthy.

After graduating with honors but suffering emotionally from a broken engagement, she ventured out west with a friend, settling in a city in the Arizona desert. Within a few short months, through a confluence of unlikely circumstances, Henry Perchfield Richardson came into her life. When they met, bells rang. He was the right one for her – kind, outgoing and a complement to her introversion, respectful, and most of all, in need of her. Religious, but not to a fault, although he preferred taking communion in his seat, not at the front with everyone else, so she left behind her Methodist upbringing and agreed to become a

Presbyterian. He had specific opinions about how properly to commune with his God. They instantly knew they were meant for one another and married after a six-week courtship.

As she made a new life for herself, Helen could almost forget those painful times with her father. She would praise him for keeping the family together after her mother's suicide, and for encouraging all of his daughters to go to high school, an unusual thing in those days. And she concluded that he had done the right thing, the moral thing, to give the family a chance to forget the traumatic horrible day when she and her sisters discovered Mother's body. If humiliating her was his major fault, duty was his strength.

The importance of fulfilling one's duty got absorbed unconsciously and translated itself into a large part of Helen's *modus operandi*. It was embedded in her psyche so fiercely that it disrupted her ability to express affection and love toward her children, even though she did love them without question. Driven by a strong sense of obligation, she banished fleeting thoughts of abandoning the marriage when Henry's obsession with discovering gold drove their finances to near-death. Duty, duty, duty was everything to Helen.

⁂

When Henry returned in two days, he had some news. "I talked to some guys near where I was prospecting. They said they just heard on the radio that a munitions dump had blown up. That's what you saw the other morning."

"Well, I read the paper and there was nothing – I mean nothing – about it," Helen sniffed.

In years to come, anyone who paid attention would learn the facts, hidden from the public to soothe the anxiety of the populace – perilous material left at the scientific laboratory north of them, polluted pools near the uranium mines several miles to the west, and nuclear warheads stored in the mountain range east of their home. There had been rumors that the actual bomb had traveled unassembled through their town heading toward the Trinity site where its first test was conducted on Helen's ordinary day.

But knowledge of these things might not have made a difference, for such happenings, known or unknown, failed to penetrate into this family's personal world, not even when later in August two Japanese cities got decimated by bombs so terrible that one could only imagine the havoc they created. Life in this one family went on in its regular way as if nothing unusual had happened. If anything, Helen was more bothered about Henry's escapades than the radioactive fallout from the peculiarly shaped cloud she saw on an early morning in July.

Helen's anxiety about her husband's continual search for a new mine and her own struggle to keep food on the table had loomed greater than the importance of what might be going on in the war or under their noses in a remote part of New Mexico. They had all missed the fact that notable scientists in a lab seventy-five miles to the north of them had been working on the creation of a weapon that would forever change the world.

War may have been distant, yet news of it came into their home every evening as they gathered round to listen to *The March of Time* on the Crosley tabletop walnut radio. Announcers boomed out the war news. At the local theater, *Movietone News* featured pictures of soldiers shooting, airplanes careening downward and sometimes exploding in mid-air. The local paper ran cartoons of bombs dropping from planes, along with ads promoting the sale of war bonds and the planting of victory gardens. But not until after the war in Europe ended did anyone in this family or their town, or in many parts of the nation, grasp the horror of the unspeakable deeds of Hitler, his killing of the Jews, the gas chambers and all the rest.

Helen would live long enough to recall the day when she witnessed the mushroom cloud emerging from the explosion at White Sands near Alamogordo. Much later, she recognized how she had circled in her own orbit, unaware of the significance. How the quotidian details of her life overtook matters that were soon to be magnified on a vast screen of cataclysmic historic events. How she had been preoccupied with dealing with her husband's absences, fixing meals, sewing dresses and bookkeeping for her husband's business. How she had fretted because she knew that he was squandering his time and their money. How that day, her young daughter Linda had heard something about fetishes and spirits and magic and precious stones and becoming rich. How she had sighed knowing that chicken dinners that would be eaten only by the two of them while her husband traipsed off somewhere to mine for ore. How she had smothered the occasional thought of escaping this marriage, just as she had escaped the family into which she was born. How she had thought it was just another mundane day. A perfectly ordinary day.

Chapter Six
Rowing Alone

After returning from the service, Shirley and Linda began early preparations for supper later that evening. Their mother sat in her favorite chair staring ahead. There were no tears. She did not speak. Then her eyes fluttered closed. She was quiet, distant, far away somewhere. The minutes, measured by the kitchen wall clock in the shape of a rooster, ticked by awkwardly.

Shirley chattered away about her three children as she moved about the kitchen. Linda could not tell whether Shirley was thinking about their father, to whom she was much closer in spirit than Linda. But Shirley had been gone for many years, and she was caught up in the duties of rearing her family in another state.

The friendly people at the church reception had departed and returned to their lives. There was emptiness now. Their lively, spirited, if self-absorbed father no longer would fill the spaces in the rooms with his opinions, his admonitions, his quirky predictions. Surely her mother must be grateful, Linda speculated, that he had suffered no major debilitating illness. Helen Richardson's practical side always took over in times of crisis. She shifted in her seat and spoke in a clear tone.

"Now I'm going to say this only once. I know you will find this difficult to believe, but the last few years were the happiest of our lives. We were very close, closer than when you two were growing up." Her face lit up in a radiance that seemed incongruous, given the circumstances.

Exchanging glances with Shirley, Linda wondered what would come next. Silence reigned. Linda felt like a rubber band being stretched too tight, ready to snap back.

That was as much admission as Linda would ever get from her mother, an implication that the years when she needed her parents the most were filled with disappointment and dismay, with dreams shattered and illusions punctured. She had wished many times that her mother, with her education, skills and work experience, would leave the marriage. But hearing what her mother had to say, she understood. This had been a commitment of sixty years. Her parents had walked through a bumpy life together, with hopes frequently unfulfilled, and yet had found moments in their marriage, at the beginning and toward the end, laced with laughter and tears, tenderness and love.

Linda pulled lettuce leaves and snapped them into bite-sized pieces, tossing together a salad. She placed the bowl in the refrigerator and helped her mother get up and move toward the table to look at pictures with Shirley. Emotions that could not rise to the surface during the service now threatened to overtake her. She did not want to give into them in front of her mother and sister.

"If it's all right with you two, I'm going to rest a bit, but I'll come back in a little while and help finish up closer to dinnertime."

Instead of going to the bedroom, she walked around the corner, out of sight, into the living room where the voices of Shirley and her mother began to fade from her hearing. She eased herself into a comfortable easy chair, propped a pillow behind her head, closed her eyes and let the memories drift in and out.

After the kitten episode, despite her mother's protests, her father insisted on moving away to a neighborhood on the outskirts of town. His reasons were never entirely clear, but the family was settled in by early summer. By any standard, this house was not nearly as adequate as the one near the church. Images appeared of her mother on hands and knees scrubbing dirt from the peeling brown linoleum and dusting the spider webs clinging to the window frames, where cracked rivulets of too many coats of paint streamed down and across the lumpy wood.

Although the front yard stretching to the unpaved street had grass and a cherry tree, the dirt backyard was unfenced, not like the house closer to town. One scraggly elm shaded the south window by her parents' bedroom, but it was not sturdy enough to support a swing.

Linda had to use her imagination. She proceeded to enlist some of the neighborhood girls her own age to join her in pretending that their mud pies were real ones, and setting out imaginary meals upon an imaginary table. They drew hop scotch squares with sticks, tossing pieces of colored glass to see whether they would land inside a chosen square. They jumped rope and played hide and seek. During bad weather, they retreated to her living room and played cards designed in sets of authors, musical composers or world capitals. By the time she was seven, Linda had lists of these categories running around in her brain. Other pastimes included checkers or jacks and outfitting paper dolls with fashions cut from catalogs or discarded magazines. A favorite game that appealed to her play group of neighborhood girls was assuming the role of current movie stars and making up plays about them. Sometimes they would quarrel over who got to be June Allison or Virginia Mayo. Some episodes were created from memory of the movies they'd seen; at other times, they spun out a script spontaneously.

A solo activity was stringing wooden beads on shoe laces. Her aunt had sent her a set. Linda was not as interested in crafts as she was in words, but she enjoyed making necklaces of infinite patterns, arranging and re-arranging the red, yellow, blue, pink and purple beads.

Movies became a favorite diversion. Her parents finally let her walk with a friend to the movie theater every week. At first, they allowed her to see only Disney animated films. *Pinocchio, Bambi* and *Snow White* all had moral or life messages, so her parents approved of these. She especially loved *Fantasia*, swept away by the story, thrilled by the background musical score, which she would later learn was from Beethoven's Sixth (Pastoral) Symphony. As her first introduction to classical music, this piece set the stage for a life-long attraction to her favorite musical genre.

After the *Movietone News* came a short feature which preceded the regular movie, a series called *Nyoka the Jungle Girl*. Nyoka was the daughter of a doctor who had come to Africa to escape his evil twin brother. She was a spunky heroine, but unlike Tarzan's Jane, Nyoka was not dressed in animal skins, but rather, regular shorts and a cotton shirt. Natives murdered her father and wanted to eliminate her, also, for they believed she had a secret amulet. Each episode ended in a harrowing experience, but she always got rescued in the next episode, only to get involved in yet another escapade. The amulet – the thing that protected her – remained in Nyoka's safekeeping. Linda was enthralled. This woman was a powerful heroine. Girls could do exciting and daring things, too, but their exploits could lead them into danger, from which they need to be rescued by men. That message got absorbed fast.

The move to this house brought no relief from the condition of being the outsider. They were the only Anglo family on the block. Next door lived the landlord and his wife, with three sons a few years older than Linda. The back yard was not only a play area, but the site of a clothesline. Linda's assigned chore was to hang up the just-washed clothes. One day as she did that, the brothers began to hurl rocks at her along with that foreign word from before, "Gringa! Gringa!" She understood its meaning but not the hate behind it. There were times in those years when she wished her skin was not so fair, her eyes not so blue, her face not sprinkled with freckles. In later years, she learned from her mother that her father had spoken to the next-door family. The stones, but not the glares, stopped.

This time in their lives could have opened the way to appreciating a different culture, but it became instead an era of missed opportunities. Although her father spoke fluent Spanish learned in the Rio Grande Valley of Texas, he did not wish that Linda take up the language, nor did her mother. The neighbors sometimes sent over bowls of chili with tortillas, which were quietly disposed of in the trash. They once invited her family to a pig roast, but her parents thanked them politely, declining as graciously as they knew how.

Her parents referred to them within the privacy of their home as "the Spanish," since they had been told that that calling them "Mexicans" would be an insult, a put-down. Her parents did not wish to complicate their existence or inadvertently communicate the wrong message to the people living within their midst. Linda's life swirled around trying to navigate the world in a sea of brown faces and nuances of another language and set of habits. She never quite grasped what should be said or not spoken.

Things came to a head one day when Linda came home from school asking innocently, "Mama, what does 'ca-ca' mean?" What should have engendered some humor instead brought on a lecture about scatological terms. After a cursory explanation that left no uncertainty in Linda's mind as to the answer, her mother spoke tartly, making what was once mild disapproval of learning Spanish now a restriction.

"And also, don't ever call me Mama. It's 'Mother.' Our name is Richardson, not Sanchez."

Into this household came a baby sister when Linda was almost seven. Now the neighborhood children, boys and girls, flocked to their house to see the new arrival. Giggling and chirping, they pointed at her, calling her "Gorda! Gringuita gorda!" To be sure, Shirley was a pudgy baby. But their faces showed that the words were uttered with fondness, not in the same tone at all as the hate-filled "Gringa!" hurled at her on several occasions.

Meanwhile, life treated her father well. He presented his face to the outside world as a charming, charismatic extrovert, popular in the community. It seemed that in every organization he joined, he immediately got tagged as a leader. On the other hand, her mother, overburdened with the entire responsibility of two children and a quixotic husband, became increasingly strict and authoritarian, and the tension spilled out in many ways into their daily lives. Linda began to bite her nails and the soft tissue around them.

As her father's absences increased in frequency, Linda would find her mother weeping while slicing carrots or cutting up a chicken for stew, or bringing in milk from the porch. Sometimes she discovered her mother pedaling furiously on her Singer sewing machine, pushing and twisting cheap cotton fabrics under the metal foot, stitching the pieces together. There was the rat-a-tat-tat of the needle puncturing the cloth that would become miraculously a yellow dotted Swiss Sunday dress and maybe even a small matching outfit for her doll. That was her mother, always keeping things together while worrying that things would come apart.

Sensitive to the atmosphere in the household, Linda absorbed the prevailing mood. By the time she reached the third grade, she began to write stories and poems illustrated with eyes and eyelashes drawn with dripping tears. Her days were filled with a series of microspasms, and between them there hung over her, like a black cloud, an inconsolable sense of loneliness.

By 1948, her father's business was failing. Her mother lost patience easily as she attempted to take care of household duties and maintain a routine. Unhappiness and uncertainty reigned in the household. Shirley was a toddler, and Linda was in third grade, escaping into a world of reading and listening to Saturday morning radio shows.

For Linda, this was the year of the willow stick, applied viciously to her bare legs when she did not return from a friend's house at the appointed time. It was the year of reading Baba Yaga stories in her Jack and Jill magazines, fantasizing that her mother had turned into the deformed witch who flew around wielding a mortar and pestle and dwelled in a house mounted on chicken legs. It was the year of town break-ins when her father's precious collection of 35 mm slides of desert flowers got stolen. It was the year of a measles outbreak during which Linda fell gravely ill, saved only by a house call from the local doctor who prescribed a relatively new drug, sulfa. It was the summer when the community pool was closed because of polio cases, and it was the Christmas of scarcity, in which Linda and her sister each received a new blouse and one orange, purchased with borrowed money from an aunt.

It was the year of the car accident, when her father, returning the family from church, made a left turn into a parking space in front of his business store front, only to be sideswiped by a car roaring down Main Street at sixty miles per hour, or so the policeman informed them afterwards. Seat belts did not exist. Linda's head flew through the back window shattering the glass, and her mother got thrown roughly against the inside passenger door. Her father held onto the steering wheel and escaped without injury, then rushed them all to the local hospital where Linda needed stitches above her eyebrow, and her mother was found to have suffered several broken ribs. Linda could not remember how they got through the next few months without her mother's steady hand keeping everything afloat.

Most significantly, it was the year when Linda's grandmother arrived. Linda had never known any grandparents. Her father's father had died before she was born. Her mother's mother was no longer in the picture, and her maternal grandfather had no interest in coming west to visit, which, Linda learned later, was a great relief to her mother who had no desire to revisit unpleasant memories of a less than satisfactory relationship.

Now eight, Linda anxiously awaited the arrival of her father's mother, who was coming to stay with them. This woman had been left destitute after the death of her husband and survived by traveling and staying a few months in each of the homes of her various children, then making the rounds again. Apparently, it was her father's turn. But Linda knew nothing of these things at that time, her grandmother's troubled history with its patient endurance of poverty and the shame of having to impose on her children.

After a few months of living with the family in their all too crowded house, Linda's father located an apartment down the street along with a live-in caretaker. Linda was allowed to stop for a visit after walking home from school. She conjured up visions of after-school cookies and milk and someone who would listen without distraction. That was rare now that her mother was tending to baby Shirley. Letting her fantasies balloon, Linda created in her mind a grandmother that did not exist.

She wanted to tell her grandmother about the things looming as supremely important – that her friend Lydia had mounds of black hair standing straight up on her head so that she appeared taller than all of the third graders but was discovered to have lice; that Sharon had kissed a boy at recess and caused an uproar; that Margaret had agreed to be her partner on the teeter-totter but then jumped off purposely so that Linda would plunge to the ground and acquire a sore backside.

Linda had hoped to share with her grandmother the litany of her school day, the markedly common experiences that were the center of her life. She wanted to talk about the boys jabbering in Spanish, brown and white together playing war games using slender tree limbs for guns, and girls on the go-round clinging to one another and the iron bars, screeching as the world flew by, their hair flying, minds whirling. But she never got the chance to share even one piece of her life, for her grandmother babbled constantly about her aches and pains and the troubles of family members that Linda had never met.

The frantic knock came early in the morning, while it was still dark.

"Mr. Richardson," a voice cried out, "your mother is awful sick!"

Linda jumped out of bed and raced to her parents' bedroom to find her father pulling on his trousers. But before he could grab his jacket and leave, a second knock came, even more urgently than before.

"Oh, Mr. Richardson! I think your mother has died!"

Linda's father took her to the funeral home to view the body. Her mother declined to go along. She said she wanted to remember her mother-in-law as she had been when she was alive. Her grandmother was dressed in soft gray wool, her gray hair neatly curled. In folded hands, she held a pink rose. Linda held her father's hand and looked up to discover tears glistening in his eyes.

"Did she go to heaven?" Linda asked.

"Your grandmother worshipped God and followed the Ten Commandments and loved Jesus. Of course, her spirit is in heaven."

"Where is heaven, Daddy?"

"It's – uh – well, where God is, and Jesus and all the angels."

"Do the angels have harps and sit on clouds?" Linda tried to imagine heaven as she had seen in pictures shown in Sunday school. "Will Grandmother get to see Jesus?"

Linda's father reached for her hand and turned his face once again to the still, peaceful woman lying in a satin-lined casket. Gazing into his face, she noticed the drawn lips, and the eyes, sad and shining.

"I – I – oh, well, it's time to say goodbye," he said softly, leaving her questions unanswered.

Linda was sad that her grandmother was no longer with them, but one bright spot served to lift her spirits. An aunt arrived from California to help with the arrangements of sending her grandmother's body back to Texas for burial. Linda had just received a small autograph book on previous birthday and asked her aunt to write something. Linda treasured this message for many years. "I saw a lively, bright, pig-tailed little girl with snapping blue eyes, full of curiosity and wonderment." Linda walked around in a daze, hanging on to those words, for not only were they the first expression of praise she had ever received, they were an abrupt departure from the critical words from her mother for not doing things perfectly and the non-responsiveness of her father.

Looking back, she realized that she had inflated the importance of the mundane events of her school day and put too much emphasis on the praise from her aunt. She had not considered the possibility that this relative might tell approximately the same thing to other nieces. Still, the message in the autograph book had fed her hopes and secret dreams for excitement, adventure, pretty dresses and public recognition for something – anything to banish the dullness of her existence, to bring some color into her life.

Although her mother must have known what was coming, Linda was shocked by the announcement that they would be moving back to Albuquerque. Up to now, her father as community paragon had been able to secure loans from the local bankers to keep the business going. But the debt got out of hand, and they could not make even the interest payments on the note. Linda was too young then to understand the details, but that explained why Christmas had been so spare and why, toward the end, they had to borrow money from her father's sister to buy groceries.

"I'm sorry to tell you this, but we'll have to sell the piano," her mother said, hugging her tightly to assuage the grief over yet one more loss.

Her mother had acquired an oak upright when the Baptist church had advertised that it was seeking a home for its piano since they were replacing it with a baby grand. She even managed for Linda to take lessons from someone who offered to teach without charging. Linda learned quickly and delighted in showing off her mastery of simple melodies. But the piano had to go. The ache in her gut on the day the movers shuffled it out the door remained for a long time.

They left in January when Linda was halfway through her fourth grade year in school. Loath to declare bankruptcy, intent on keeping their good name, her parents determined to pay off the debt. The family spent the next seven years making loan payments, barely scraping by.

Linda never was certain how it happened, given the cloud hanging over their heads, but her father somehow negotiated the purchase of a modest house, assuming a note costing them monthly about the same amount as a rented property would be. It had two bedrooms and a cellar where her mother could store what she canned during the growing season: jars of peaches, plums, beans, peas and corn. In the cellar was a tiny space framed in by the previous owner, a secret place into which Linda dragged a folding chair, retreated with her books, and hung up posters of her favorite movie stars. She had to take a flashlight with her since there were no electrical outlets.

She began to grasp that there was an outer world – confusing, duplicitous and rule-bound, to which she had to conform – and her inner world, which presented as both logical and magical, filled with stories about many kinds of people, with poetry and music and limitless dreams and ambitions. It was a small and tender world, easily shattered by personal disappointments, yet at the same time oblivious to the sufferings in the world at large.

Linda was sorry that her sister and she were too far apart in age to be close companions. Then, there was the matter of their disparate personalities. The two sisters responded to their father in diametrically opposite ways. Shirley demanded to have things her own way, fighting back against the household rules. And their father admired her for it. He overtly showed his favoritism to Shirley. With money so hard to come by, Linda resented that he would hand over cash to Shirley to treat herself and her friends to hamburgers and ice cream sodas. It fell to Linda to earn her own way; not one penny was offered, ever, even if asked for. Shirley, clearly, in Linda's view, was the favored child. Although her sister was not the cause of her (Linda's) being shunted aside, it was hard to avoid jealousy directed toward Shirley and fury aimed at her father.

As the days rolled on, she often forgot these negative emotions in the living of an average, outward day-to-day existence. There were barefoot treks over dusty roads, sunburned shoulders, Kool-aid swigs for thirst quenchers, friendships lost and made – all the normal and ordinary events of the pre-teen years, many of them shaped by living in the Southwest. She endured the dryness of those days, but her dreams were of rivers and lakes and oceans on which she saw herself adrift, rowing alone. Alone, yes, but trusting her inner world, along with some adored teachers and a few close friends, to steer her through the shoals.

※

After working briefly at several sales jobs, but knowing that he was better suited for running his own show, her father established himself again in business. For a while, tension eased in the family, but then it escalated again to new heights. Her father had not lost the taste for treasure hunting. He had been to a card reader again, and her mother's temper surged. This time, she set down the boundaries. Stop the mining ventures, or you will have to leave.

Linda was aware of their quarrels and her mother's efforts to supplement the family income at home. Extra money was never available. By the time she was twelve, Linda started babysitting and saving her money. By the time she reached high school, she was buying her own clothes, purchasing bus tokens to get to school and paying her church pledge.

She was a devoted student and a voracious reader. Her mother was a devotee of the English poets and also American writers, especially Mark Twain and Edgar Allen Poe. She encouraged Linda to read widely but then fumed when Linda became obsessed with the Nancy Drew mystery series. Linda began to write poems and essays and summaries of the books she read to keep track of the ideas that were now exploding in her brain. She fell in love with classical music when her fifth grade teacher played for them, among others, Bizet's *L'Arlesienne Suite*, Grieg's *Peer Gynt Suite* and Respighi's *Pines and Fountains of Rome*.

Music in the home had been limited to exposure to popular hits. Before the move to Albuquerque, one of the rare family activities that the four of them shared was listening to the "Hit Parade" on the radio. They took turns guessing which one would be Number One on the charts each week. One of her favorites was "Nature Boy" sung by Nat King Cole. But her father objected to the song. He said that the song was suggesting that the nature boy was Jesus Christ. That was a sacrilege, her father said, for no one should be compared to Jesus, who was divine. Linda wondered if she was committing some kind of sin to like this song. She let its words and music play over and over silently in her head, wondering why the things that attracted her often were rejected by her father.

When she got to ninth grade, she signed up for first year Latin. The first phrase she learned was *Ad astra per aspera* – "To the stars through difficulties."

⁂

Somewhere along the path in her journey to understand her father, she concluded that he was basically a well-meaning man who believed strongly that he cared deeply for his family. That he might have caused damage or hurt would never have entered his mind. His focus was so relentless that he moved through his days undaunted and unabated, but the singular pursuit of his own happiness trumped anyone else's.

Linda idolized him and yearned for his affection, his guidance, his respect for her as she grew into womanhood. She was gradually learning to live without her father's attention, but she always hoped against hope that something she did would make him proud of her. Her solution was to become the perfect child. She attended church faithfully, recited the Apostle's Creed each Sunday, sang in the church choir, worked hard to earn straight A's, made friends with bright and talented young people.

Her mother remained a stalwart source of support, although much of her attention was diverted into the care of her sister Shirley. To gain recognition, Linda pushed herself toward academic achievement, discovering that teachers could be surrogate parents when it came to praise.

Still, the troubles at home persisted. When Linda was eleven with fast-growing limbs that made her stumble about, she was on hand to help her father varnish the woodwork in their tiny living room. Her father, busily engaged in his task, asked her to bring him a rag. She jumped up to fetch it and did not see the lamp cord still attached to the socket. Her shoe caught the cord and pulled the lamp to the wood floor, shattering it in all directions.

"You clumsy oaf!" he cried out.

As the years passed, those searing words no longer throbbed. But inwardly, she had buried a casket of rage and resentment, absorbing well his message, as she interpreted it, that she was not worthy of being remembered or recognized. Doubts about her competence, abilities and femininity assailed her as she grew into adolescence and then into womanhood.

※

Early on, Linda had questioned the reason for the lack of closeness. She wondered what was wrong with her that made him so distant. Why did he forget her birthday periodically? There had been two new Bibles, one on her seventh birthday, the other on her fifteenth, but little else in between. On occasion, in a last minute gesture, he would come up belatedly with some sort of gift, usually from his own possessions. Once when she was nineteen, she received a hot water bottle, not new but something he was discarding, wrapped in tissue paper. As he handed it to her, his mouth twitched in that familiar way, showing that he obviously was pleased with himself. Later, seeing that facial expression made her irritated and resentful, even when she knew that her father meant well.

Gifts given should be acknowledged, her mother taught her. Say to the person how much you value them. So, as a dutiful daughter, she thanked him, playing the game well. But the gesture was seldom returned. Too many times, her gifts to him were cast aside or he would say that he already had whatever it was that she had picked out, leaving her feeling rebuffed. After so many years, she expected her offerings to be rejected and eventually decided to send only a card of well-wishes on his birthday or other occasions. As an adult, she would agonize over something purchased for a friend. If it wasn't just the right thing, she sweated that would it be spurned, or at the least, damned with faint praise.

Once in her teen years, after she got a part-time job, she bought a gift she thought her father would enjoy. It was a book entitled *The Family of Man* featuring a massive set of photographs first shown in an exhibit at the New York City Museum of Modern Art. With his avid interest in photography, surely he would like this. Some time later, he said he wanted to talk to her. He said that it was filthy and that she should not be seeing such things. Astounded, she begged for an explanation.

"It's that picture of the black woman," he said. "I won't show it to you; you know which one."

Mystified, Linda scoured the book and found what probably had set off her father's moralistic admonition. There was one picture, a head shot of an African-American woman's face, partially covered by the back of a man's head. Her expression glowed right off the page; her visage indicated that she was in ecstasy. Linda was too ashamed to discuss the matter with her mother. Out of all this wonderful collection, her father had found the one he thought would be detrimental to her moral character. After that, she stopped giving him presents.

Over the course of her school years, she found herself wishing for a different sort of paternal parent. She was taught that envy was one of the seven deadly sins. Yet, questions persisted. Why couldn't he be like Catherine's father, one who would inquire about what was going on in school, who guided her expertly into courses she would need for college, who had the money to send her there? Or Annette's, a General in the U.S. Army, who shared his knowledge on everything from finance to desert plants? Or Marilyn's, who would listen to her intently, who regarded her as young person with talents and abilities?

She expended huge quantities of emotional energy to prove to herself that he was not the worst of all fathers. After all, he did not leave the family. He was not a drunkard, like Alice's father. He did not have tuberculosis like Deborah's father. He did not divorce her mother as happened in Sharon's family. He did not beat up on his children. Norma had shared that secret; Linda had noticed that Norma missed so much school. There were even whispers that Norma endured more than just beatings, that her father was "having" her. Those were shocking revelations, for she could not imagine a father doing such harm to a daughter. He did not have a debilitating illness, like that in Evelyn's family. Evelyn had to race home from school to perform caretaking duties for her seriously ill father while her mother left for a job to support the family. Nor had her father died, as Jolene's father, leaving six children and a wife to fend for themselves.

"You have a pretty good deal," some of those friends had said. The implication was that she should not feel such pain about his disregard. Or embarrassment at his boring monologues foisted on any friend who would visit. Or shame because of her shabby surroundings.

She resented how someone else could judge another's psychic pain or disappointments. No one could predict how early rejection by a father figure might affect one's choices later in life, or comprehend how that situation – call it a dragon – could burrow underground and hide in one's subconscious. It slid around in there and occasionally surfaced, displaying its flashing tail when irritated by life events both momentous and minor. She finally came to accept the validity of her own feelings and rejected the idea of placing various traumas on some sort of scale, weighing and comparing them, so that someone could confidently pronounce, "Mine was more horrible than yours, so you have nothing to complain about."

She and her father were star-crossed personalities, doomed by nature, patterned by nurture, never to understand each other. In that conundrum lay the seeds of a hidden unhappiness that never completely resolved itself. Sometimes she thought she would never figure out what made her father tick.

But over time, through a long learning process, she came to understand that *she* was not entirely the problem. Her father simply was wrapped up in himself. Understanding that helped her choose to accept him and his ways, but at the same time acknowledge her own self-worth.

The beads strung in childhood were like the moments of her life, growing into hours, into days and finally into years. The resulting necklaces, she now thought, must have represented an attempt to develop some order, some meaning, some pattern to explain her surreal world. All it took to shatter this illusion of an orderly existence was to snip the shoelace and watch the beads scatter, banging into one another as they rolled across the floor, back into chaos.

❧

"Linda, would you set the table?" Shirley's voice startled her out of her reverie.

With a sigh, she arose and walked around the corner to the kitchen to help her widowed mother get through the rest of the evening.

Desert Daughter

Part Two

When you're young, you think everything you do is disposable. You move from now to now, crumpling time up in your hands, tossing it away. You're your own speeding car. You think you can get rid of things, and people too – leave them behind. You don't yet know about the habit they have, of coming back.

—Margaret Atwood, *The Blind Assassin*

Chapter Seven
Mood of the Dunes

The golden moments in the stream of life rush past us, and we see nothing but sand; the angels come to visit us, and we only see them when they are gone.
      —George Eliot
        (Mary Ann Evans, English novelist, 1819-1880)

In that earlier time, they came upon the dunes near a beach campground and claimed them for their own with wonder and awe like ancient explorers discovering a new world. They were a family, this mother, father and child. There was silent communion in this place, and the bonds had tightened. They had been pirates then, stealing memories instead of gold. But the treasure had dwindled and could not be replaced.

They had headed toward the ocean, pulling their blue nylon windbreakers closer, walking over the beach dunes leading to the shore. Grasses fluttered just above the ground and clouds raced through a dazzling sky. The sand was smooth and silky, not gritty and hot like desert soil. Together, they stooped to pull tufts of sea grass and flung the dried stalks over the rippling brown silt so fine that if they wished, they could walk barefoot. The scent of sea life filled their nostrils, to remain there in memory of this magical place. Ahead, the waves pounded the shore. They rose in ear-drumming crescendos, then fell into soft splashes, endlessly repeating the rhythm of rising and falling and splashing.

The man encircled her with his arm to keep them both warm. She slid her own arm around his waist and they looked knowingly at each other, smiling, believing their love was secure. The child ran ahead, leaping with joy. He chased after her and suddenly the two of them were running toward the surf, pausing only to strip to swim suits underneath their clothes. The woman watched as they waded into the water and began splattering each other. The child squealed with delight. "Come in! It's fun!" he yelled to her. She waved and smiled back at them but shook her head. Instead, she shed her sandals and dug her toes into the ooze near the shoreline. The tide was out, and she was content to sit a while with the hermit crabs, the clamshells and the sand dollars.

Idly, she began to construct a sand castle. Build it now, she thought. At high tide, it will be no more. Molding the moist sand, she could not have believed nor have predicted the crumbling of their lives that was to come. So confident was she of their love that she saw no harm in staying separate for a while. After a while, the two left the water and joined her. Together, all three stretched out and lay baking on the sand until the sun spilled molten liquid into the surf and dipped away.

But in the course of their daily lives that followed, conflicts arose and recriminations reigned. Scenes escalated and subsided, rising and falling like the undulating dunes. Too many misunderstandings, too few apologies. Patterns locked, and a time came when indifference seeped into the relationship. There were wounds left with words, and wounds made because of no words.

Trepidation, doubt and guilt gripped her. She wanted to grow; he was happy for things to remain static. Her attempts to describe her feelings to him met resistance. And so, the closeness of the early years slipped slowly away, moving imperceptibly at first until a wide gulf opened between them and neither knew how to mend the rift.

Her hunger to recapture those early feelings drove her to visit the dunes with the two of them a second time, hoping for the place itself to reclaim riches lost, yearning for the memories to re-ignite passions faded, to mend heartstrings now tattered.

It was here so long ago, but really not so long ago, that they stood in a frozen moment of eternity when there existed an illusory belief that their lives would remain forever in the throes of connectedness, of passion, of love. Here was the spot where nothing would ever change, nothing would ever disturb their lives. Yet, she should have noticed that here the great God Triton left sand deposits to be turned into heaps of undulating hills, shaped by the washing of the eternal sea.

Things appear to be the same, she notices, now with this second visit. Just as before, the grasses on the dunes flutter in the breeze. Just as before, the breakers crash near the shore. Separately, they move onto the dunes, not holding hands like last time, each pushed in a different direction by the roaring wind. Her child, older now, cartwheels down a silken slope.

"Watch me!" she calls to her father. He follows his daughter, catches her from behind and lifts her above his head so that her legs clutch around his neck. Then, bending his knees, he turns her out gently upon the sand. She giggles, struggling to her feet. Then she lies down on the dune, fluttering her arms and legs like a jumping jack.

"Look, I'm an angel, just like before!" calls the little girl.

"Or a butterfly," remarks the mother. The sand impression unmistakably suggests a pair of wings.

He tramps along, testing the pressure of the sand against his shoes with the ever-blowing ocean breeze. He likes to be alone, to compete against the wind and conquer it. She does not reach for his hand, though the bones of her fingers are chilled.

Ripples of sand weave and sway just yards from the vast expanse of the mighty sea. The surf pounds and recedes, regular in its rhythm. The dunes heave and curve, shaped and re-shaped by the never-ending western wind into burial mounds for banished sea life, silent graves covered with thin, thirsty grasses.

She stoops for a clam shell, an enormous one, completely intact, perfectly hinged. Fingering its smooth, porcelain-like surface, she ponders. So utterly matched, these fans. So protective, yet the silent inhabitant has long since disappeared. It is a bi-valve, she notes, two parts. Click open, slam shut. Like castanets clacking in her brain. She wrestles with the two parts, the push-pull of looking back at another time that maybe never was, and the moving forward out of her own shell, pressing past fears and doubts.

"Here!" she signals to her daughter, "for your collection." She tosses the shell and the child runs forward, grabs it and stuffs it in her pocket.

"Oh, I'll keep it forever! It won't change, will it, Mommy?"

They duck their heads as the wind whips their faces, aglow from the salt air swirling about them, and continue walking toward the mighty ocean, a vagabond trio. At the crest of a knoll, they pause to take notice of a refuge for seabirds nestled between two sections of dunes. Gulls dip and sway above this marshy spot, zoning in for food and protection. It is a swampy, grassy area, tucked away between the dunes, a source of nourishment for myriad forms of life.

She is far behind but matches her pace to the others'. Her spine tingles, for the breeze off the water brings a chill. Yes, it all looks as it did before. But it isn't the same. Turning her head, she sees that the tread of their feet has altered, ever so slightly, the configuration of the sand. Tufts of grass sway beneath her feet. Salt crystals lash her tongue. And somewhere in the marsh, the wild birds wail desolate cries. Shivering, she tucks her hands inside her sweater and holds herself close, close to her own body.

"There's a fish," her husband says, pointing, for they had played a game that other time, imagining the shapes of the dunes. Perhaps he, too, recalls the earlier time when they came, before strife took over. Perhaps he, too, feels the slippage. "Here's a whale," announces the daughter, dragging her fingers through the tawny powder to simulate the spray from the blow hole.

"I need a rest," she calls over the roar of wind and sea. "Go ahead, I'll stay here for a while." It does not elude her that this is the second time she has withdrawn. She finds a rock high enough to climb where she can clearly view the marsh, the dunes and ocean. Dreamily, the water birds loop the sky, swoop over sand and water. She spots her daughter and husband ascending, leaping up the hill ahead. When they reach the top, they celebrate their victory. Her child's laughter ripples over the dunes. Dappled light cascades upon the shore. The sound travels over the valley where the shore birds nest. Between the space where she is perched and the other two lies a chasm of shifting sand.

She turns partially around, her back to the wind, and huddles herself close again, pulling her jacket over the back of her neck and holding it tightly against her throat. Across the valley of sand, her daughter climbs a hill of sea grass. She has outdistanced her father, and he races to catch up. They rollick and tease, oblivious to all but the wind in their faces. They are a raucous pair.

The wind grows even colder, and she sees the moon rising, a faint white globe in the southern sky. The sun, not yet set, blazes upon the dunes and pierces the ocean. The rolling waters shimmer, stabbed by punctures of fast-sinking light.

Her thoughts whirl. They are the takers of the moment, she thinks, but I worry about preserving time. She stays distant, holding a memory, not willing to release it, hoping for the same feeling to come again. She sees now the futility of trying to cling to them, because she is changing, evolving, growing new armor. She thinks again of the clamshell. Open, shut. Forward, back. It is difficult, this birth.

They are together, chasing, embracing the joy and exhilaration of the day. She is alone, observing, hoping and waiting for the closeness to come again. She stands between the sun and the moon, the ocean and the top of the hill. The wind and sea, sun and moon, birds and marsh – all are related, moving in perfect harmony. But she has chosen to be solitary, right here, right now. She senses the difference now between loneliness and aloneness. The ocean is near; she feels its pulse like the slow rhythm of a beating heart.

The other two are coming toward her from the other hill, but everything is distorted as if they are moving away and disappearing from her sight. Her child sees her, points and smiles. Her husband brandishes his hand back and forth in the breeze. She tries to smile back, but her face is a mask pinned like a flapping paper against the wind. The wind rips over her body, and she moves her feet and fingers to restore warmth.

The shadows of the dune ridges lengthen on the moon side. The two on the hill descend, laughing and puffing. She rises to greet them. Under her shoes, the sand is moving, separating, regrouping like their lives together. Now is now; then was then, to be cherished but not repeated. She realizes she needs to go deep into her soul to find the answers to the conundrum of the clamshell, to balance two desires. Rootedness, freedom. Permanence, growth. Which will prevail and at what price?

They rush up to her, and she offers her arms. She needs their warmth, for she is very chilled. The sea birds, moaning, circle the sky, then disappear. The wind dies down; the sun bleeds into the sea. The ocean faithfully brings the waves puddled with gold, to break against the shore.

Chapter Eight
Witch's Hair

Summer, 1976

The door from the garage to the house slammed hard. Larry was home. Linda could not hear the yellow Oldsmobile pull into the garage. It was so sleek, smooth and efficient, a well-oiled machine, just like Larry. But she knew by the sound of the door what kind of day it had been. His business suit would be rumpled. It was 10 p.m.

One hour before, Linda had finished the bedtime routine with their seven-year-old daughter. Bath, pajamas, reading. *Wind in the Willows*, *Charlotte's Web*, and then *Fantasia* on the record player. Kisses, sweet dreams, Christi. Larry had been coming home later and later with each passing day. Working on a new client was all he would ever say. He breezed past her without a word and went straight to the liquor cabinet. Scotch and water, followed by another and then another. No cordial greeting, asking how her day had gone. No touching of the hands as once was their practice. He used to arrive in the early evening so that he could play with Christi.

"Where's Daddy?" Christi asked before rubbing her eyes and tucking her pillow underneath her curly head.

"I'm sure he'll be here soon and be sorry that he missed your play time." That was all she could muster up, but she knew it was a pathetic excuse and was uneasy that it just might be a lie.

Larry collapsed on the sofa and rubbed the cocktail glass. No words. No eye contact. She stared at him, noticing the beginning of creases around his eyes, the stretching of his tan skin over once-plump cheeks. His forehead, she observed, was more exposed these days. She hadn't noticed at first, but there it was. Like her love for him – inexorably slipping away, imperceptible at first, then denied, then examined, then faced as real. Their marriage was dying by degrees, just like the quiet and subtle disappearance of that once-full shock of hair, root by root – the blond hair that she used to run her hands through, smiling at him with naïve expectation that the tenderness would be permanent, would never change. Even their once passionate times together, which had kept them on an even keel, had dissolved into a pattern. No murmuring, no sharing, just Larry turning over in bed afterwards, his back to her.

"Let's go out to the pool and soak in the hot tub. It's so beautiful under the stars," she said, hoping to entice him. No answer.

When things did not go right, Linda at first blamed herself. But later, she got angry at herself that she accepted the role of solo household manager – thrust on her by Larry – without protesting. He wanted the socks rolled and stacked in the drawer in exactly a certain way and his eggs cooked perfectly, sunny side up, soft but not too soft, just enough so that he could mop up the yolk with his toast. And he did not want to be bothered by family matters. Her role was to provide for his comfort, inflate his ego and not ask for help of any kind – with Christi, the house or simply the business of day-to-day living. As she had done in childhood, she buried the resentment, fearful of Larry's retaliation if she should object or ask for his help on occasion.

Small matters escalated. Once, when they were outside heading to the backyard pool, she heard a gurgling sound.

"Is that a faucet running?" she had asked.

Larry had growled at her, "Well, go turn it off yourself – you know the house is your responsibility."

Such a little thing, a dripping faucet. Droplets of her married life going somewhere, onto the grass, forming a rivulet, becoming a stream, and if not stopped, growing into a flood. She had tried ignoring his surly moods, his churlish ways. The jaunty optimism that had attracted her to him in the first place had vanished. His work was going well, his income increasing exponentially by the year. Isn't that what he wanted, what they both had strived for? Memories of their courtship and engagement flooded in. Promises spoken and later broken – those occurred in her books, in TV soap operas, in plays and movies. Wouldn't happen to her, of course not.

What had she bought into, and why? She chided herself as she confronted her own weakness, the passive acceptance of the role that Larry had defined for her in exchange for a financially secure life, one that she had never known before. Underprivileged to overprivileged. It was a powerful draw. She now had it all – the curly-haired daughter, the house on the hillside with a view of the Pacific Ocean, the swimming pool, tasteful furnishings, the thoroughbred dog. And she was miserable.

Somewhere along the line she realized the fool's bargain. Early on, like most of her friends who came of age in the late 1950s, she had seen her major role as that of being helpmate to a career-successful husband. She had been young, easily starstruck by the ambitious business major she had met through a friend at the university. Larry was finishing a college degree on the GI Bill. She would help him climb the corporate ladder. The prospect dazzled her.

She felt she had struck a gold mine. Larry was the right man for her at that point in her life. But as with many marriages, intentions somehow never lived up to the reality of every day. Linda harbored guilt that she had not lived up to his expectations. And she redoubled her efforts to please him.

It was a bit of a shock that she had to nudge him over the edge to agree to buy their first home, ten years after they had married, just after Christi had come into their lives. She had been ready to settle down, to have a neighborhood, a community, playmates for Christi. She did not understand Larry's negative attitude. As she looked back, she admitted to a twinge of disappointment that he never got as excited as she when they finally became homeowners using his veteran's benefits to secure a no-down loan. But she had brushed it off, knowing that he applied himself diligently at his work, and she respected him for that. To be sure, he did adore Christi, but he confessed to her about eight years after the wedding that he really would have preferred that they remain childless. They had talked prior to their engagement about having a family. It was not just assumed; it was verbalized, agreed upon. Now it stole upon her that perhaps he had acquiesced to win her favor. Undoubtedly, she had missed some subtle but unmistakable reluctance.

His outward cheerfulness began to fade. He started to carp, to complain, to control. Her prior assumptions had been wrong. She thought he would wish to share joys and troubles together. Just after he proposed, he had said to her, "If we have disagreements, let's sit down and talk about them and work things out."

Linda had longed for a child. Larry was less enthusiastic but eventually gave in. Once a pink-cheeked little girl arrived, however, he seemed happy with his tow-headed, adorable daughter. They named her Christi Marie Sanders. During the first few years, they spent their weekends as a family at the park or the beach. Those were happy times. Larry and Christi had a special bond. He invented creative games to play with her, and together, they loved to splash around in the ocean near the shoreline.

Both Larry and Linda were charmed by Christi's unusual verbal ability. Once during a dinner out at a fancy restaurant, Christi saw a waiter hand Linda a chilled fork for salad and asked, "Were waiters just plain ordinary people until they were trained to be polite?"

Things changed around the time Christi was four. Larry was working late. Larry was too tired. Larry no longer enjoyed family outings on the weekends. Larry wanted to play tennis with his limited hours. He became the indulgent father, showering Christi with candy, money, stuffed animals, hats of all kinds. But Christi knew he wasn't there for her as much as before, and she began acting out in order to gain his favor and his material gifts.

Linda saw that Christi was turning into a strong-willed little tiger who insisted, "I want it my way, right here, right now." Once, Linda recalled, Christi invited her friend Shannon to come over, but then ignored Shannon in favor of playing alone with her new bunny. Shannon left, leaving a terse note that read, "I'm not your friend anymore." Christi showed no remorse or regret.

Once, Linda's friend Marilyn had brought her two children over to swim. Christi pushed water at James, spat at Colin, burped in their faces. Linda was mortified, pulled Christi out of the pool and dressed her down like a drill sergeant. She lectured Christi about manners, about how others did not like her when she behaved that way. She suspended pool privileges for several days, to no avail. Christi did not grasp that the world did not revolve around her, that she could not treat others with indignities without consequences.

Christi could always get her way with Larry, but not with Linda. Christi hurled the epithet, "You're a witch!" so often that Linda began to believe it was true. Linda reeled with self-doubt. She became depressed, afraid that despite her strong desire to be a good mother, she was failing in every way.

Linda had to admit that she was falling into the one pattern of mothering that she knew – and had determined not to repeat. Helen Richardson demanded perfection. If obedience came not swiftly, a disapproving lecture, the back of the hand, or the green willow switch produced immediate compliance. Unlike Shirley, who defied the punishments with sassing and back talk, Linda, knowing the consequences of defiance, submerged her feelings. Depending upon the incident, these ranged from minor annoyance or irritation to downright hatred. It took her years to untangle her feelings, but, once faced, there came over her a feeling of relief, as if a purging had taken place.

With Larry delegating all the difficult child-rearing to her, Linda wondered if the generations were repeating themselves. Super-critical mother; passive, indulgent father. Recipe for disaster. The similarities between Shirley and Christy could not be dismissed. Maybe Shirley, for all her bluster and bravado, was secretly insecure. Perhaps Christi, like her Aunt Shirley at an earlier time, was lost in a forest of insecurity and unhappiness and their common survival mode took the form of bullying and testing.

※

Linda wanted so much for things to be different, for Larry to acknowledge that they needed to become more in accord with their disparate parenting styles. One night they sat down for a rare meal together, one that Linda had prepared to please him. He had already consumed his usual three or four drinks before the meal started. She had prepared filet mignon, baked potato topped with chunks of butter and dollops of sour cream, and fresh artichokes she had purchased that day at the farmer's market. There would be a fine cabernet sauvignon, also.

Wading into risky territory, she ventured, "You probably have noticed that Christi is becoming a handful. I think it's partly because we aren't on the same page. You give in to her wheedling and whining."

She tried to point out to Larry that Christi's elfin ways as a six-year-old might slide into a know-it-all attitude that would not be appreciated as she grew older.

"She's great," was his response. "What's wrong with you?"

Pausing, choosing her words carefully, she said, "I agree that she's a wonderful child. She's delightful much of the time. And very bright. But the things you give her are substitutes for your presence."

Larry stacked his artichoke leaves in neat little piles on his side plate. Not one could be out place. Linda tossed hers randomly. Suddenly she thought of her mother's insistence on having everything perfectly in order – dishes stacked on shelves, not one out of place; socks mated and stacked by color and size; towels folded exactly corner to corner, not one thread hanging.

"But can't you see that she's often obnoxious when we take her places? And you just go ahead and buy her things that she demands, like the time we went to Disneyland and you promised to buy her a Mickey Mouse hat if she'd be good. Well, she drove us both crazy and wouldn't be satisfied, but you bought her the hat anyway. What kind of message does that send to her?"

"What's wrong with a Mickey Mouse hat? She looked so cute!"

Linda smothered the urge to remind him that he bought a hat for himself, too, cruising the grounds of Disneyland looking ridiculous with felt-covered mouse ears jutting from the side of his head. She suspected he was enjoying being the child he never could be, having grown up with few such pleasures. Nevertheless, she prayed that they would not run into anyone that they knew. Life was turning into a cartoon, an absurd comic book story from which she wanted to escape.

"But she doesn't really want *things* even though she begs for them. She wants you to draw the line, be her guide, show her what is proper behavior and what is not. And mostly to come home early enough to spend time with her. She's been missing you."

"She's fine," he repeated, not responding to the suggestion that he come home earlier in the evening.

"Why can't we gravitate to the center? I should be firm but not so harsh and it would help if you would be firm also and not let her insistence on having her own way wear you down so that you give in." Larry sat stone-faced.

Linda knew she should back off. She bit her lip, admitting to herself it was a mistake to bring this up during a special meal. She should have tried to create a romantic evening instead of veering off into subjects that Larry detested. But getting his attention for private conversations interfered with his playing tennis and schmoozing with business clients. She persisted, unable to stop herself from plunging into a communication disaster.

"We need to agree on consequences for Christi when she annoys other people and refuses to do her chores. Yesterday, she fed her dinner to Dudley, then asked you for money to buy junk food because she was hungry. I tried to tell you, but you wouldn't listen, and you handed her some cash. That undermines me, and I get even harsher with Christi. It's not fair to either of us."

At the sound of his name, Dudley the dachshund waddled up to the table, his belly brushing the tufts of the moss green area rug underneath the cherrywood dining table, his winsome brown eyes cast upward in hopes of receiving a little piece of steak. With the slight cocking of his head and a soft whining that none of them could resist, Larry cut a small slice and slipped it under the table.

Larry looked amused. "I think that was pretty clever of Christi. He probably enjoyed it more than that dry pellet shit he gets every day. Or maybe not. Your dinners aren't all that good most of the time, anyway."

He smiled broadly flashing a row of perfect white teeth. Linda clamped her mouth shut, grinding her molars. Either he was teasing her, or once again, insinuating that she was a less-than-perfect wife.

Bypassing the put-down for the time being, Linda tried to maneuver the conversation to a point that might force him to look down the road. "What kind of a teenager do you want? She coaxes and pleads, and you give her everything she asks for. But her desires are limitless. You may get tired of that. We don't want her to turn to drugs or worse."

Larry was now on his second glass of wine. "What I get from all of this is just too 'loosey goosey' with no management principles."

"Well, you're the business major – why don't you come up with some strategies and we'll talk about them and agree on a plan?" Linda retorted.

"The plan is that you wanted the child, now you have her, so you deal with it," he grumbled irritably.

Linda's own patience was drawing thin. She knew she had her faults; she'd admit to that. But Larry never saw himself as part of the problem. Later, in reflection, she knew that she, too, was complicit, that this was the wrong time, the wrong place to bring up these issues. But she blindly pushed forward. Suppressed needs overwhelmed good sense. Trying to muffle her exasperation, she picked up her wine glass and watched the blood-red cabernet twirl around, circling in the long-stemmed goblet.

"I just hope that Christi won't embarrass you someday. Why don't you back me up in handling her?"

"Oh, good grief!" He shook his head and put down his steak knife. "Just let me eat my supper!" Naturally, Linda thought, his answer would come from a Charles Schulz Peanuts cartoon. There it was again, the absurd upside down world of comic strips, with their bubbles displaying glib responses. So handy to quote when he wanted to whisk away any problem solving. Dudley, responsive to raised voices, barked as if trying to tell them to settle down.

Linda controlled her desire to snap at her husband. Her steak was getting cold but she pressed on even though she knew the destructive path she was taking. It was as if she were on one of those slides in the park with Christi where you gain momentum and can't stop and finally hit the dirt.

"Larry, where is our marriage going? We are beginning to tear each other apart!"

"Christi and I don't have a problem. *You* have a problem. Just don't bother me!" he practically screamed at her, scowling ferociously. Dudley barked.

"Christi's asleep, I think. I hope she doesn't hear you," Linda said in a monotone, trying to lower the temperature. She even reached out her hand, tried to touch Larry's in a gesture she hoped he would accept as a peace offering. He jerked his arm back.

Linda withdrew her hand using it to tuck a strand of auburn hair behind her ear while attempting to compose herself. Trying to remain calm, neutral, she carefully cut a piece of her steak. Then, slipping into a modulated tone, making every effort to sound rational, for Larry always accused her of being too emotional, she said, "I have trouble when you shut me out even if it's about a request you've made that I'm trying to clarify. I try to please you, but sometimes, I find it impossible to do exactly what you want when you won't elaborate." Slowly, she lifted the fork.

Larry paused and broke a roll in half, buttering it half-heartedly. "I don't expect much. You're nagging me. You're a fishwife!"

Linda held her fork in mid-air. He was always tossing off comments he had learned from his all-male company colleagues. She knew that she was nagging him, and no man would endure that or understand how it arose from sheer frustration.

Larry got up and stormed off from the table, leaving half of his dinner on the plate. "Now you've ruined my evening!"

His words hung in the air along with the beefy smell of grilled filet mignon. "I'm going to do some work!" Linda knew that he wouldn't be filing papers, but instead thumbing through his Playboy magazines.

After cutting up some bite-sized pieces of the now-cold filet to feed Dudley, Linda scraped the rest of the uneaten food into the waste basket. Her guts churned. For the comforts of life, she'd exchanged parts of her soul. Perhaps Larry was right, that she was inflating the problems. Perhaps he was justified in his criticism. He took pride that he had given her the good life, but what *was* the good life?

That night, she tried to approach him in bed, to say she was sorry for bringing up the subject of Christi. As a consequence of her unhappiness, their lovemaking had gone into a precipitous decline. The tenderness, affection and intimacy of those earlier years were missing. Larry remained oblivious. To him, nothing was amiss. While not forever gone, their love life was at low ebb. She reached out to him as he turned over, adjusting his pajama top, his back to her. She patted his shoulder tenderly as if to say with touch alone what she could not bring herself to say aloud – let's go back, start over. He shifted noticeably away from her and removed her hand. Through her tears, she saw on his cotton night clothes a blurred mass of perfect rumples, parallel valleys and hills.

***

Linda tried to sort out whether her feelings for Larry were ebbing because of the problems with Christi. But she knew that the troubles preceded Christi's entrance into their lives. She had married Larry for his stability, business acumen and work ethic. Maybe also for love, or what she thought was love at age nineteen. He wasn't the type to get involved in the unrealistic endeavors that her father fell for.

Larry had been a catch – blond, tan, muscular, the owner of a cream-colored convertible – looking for a mate. Marriage followed an eighteen-month engagement. Linda dropped out of the university and took a full-time job to support him while he finished his senior year and received his bachelor's degree. They played tennis together when he wasn't studying.

Although she could not pinpoint when their closeness began to fade, the residual feeling reminded her of a younger self when came the dawning realization that her father was edging further and further out of her life. So it was now, with her chosen spouse.

During the time before Christi, Linda had begun to develop a number of her own interests. Books were tops on her list. She kept a diary of what she read, recording phrases and new insights that helped her understand different points of view, or lyrical passages in poetry or fiction. She liked history, too, and was beginning to take an interest in various perspectives in politics. She haunted every library in each city they inhabited, carrying home stacks of books and then devouring fiction, current events, biography, psychology. Larry did not read at all except for business magazines, and he carped at her for her love of books. But she kept on reading. She tried several times to share with her husband what she was learning. He listened but looked bored.

One book that affected her deeply was Robert Pirsig's *Zen and the Art of Motorcycle Maintenance*. It spoke to her in some ways, but in others baffled her. The main character, Phaedrus, spent time pondering the meaning of Quality. He appeared to be trying to find a middle place between being too analytical and too romantic in the sense of casting all rationality and judgment to the winds. But all his inquisitiveness just led to a mental breakdown. Linda had pondered that, thinking that if Quality, whatever Pirsig meant by that term, does exist, it shouldn't lead to mental illness. Phaedrus wandered all through the thoughts of many philosophers, but where it led was to complete self-isolation. So how could that be Quality? She wrote in her book journal that she believed strongly that we do have responsibilities to others as well as ourselves. We need each other to survive. In the end, Phaedrus's son was the one who gave him the impetus to get well.

She connected the ideas to her own life. Christi was depending upon her. She loved Christi deeply but was frustrated with herself for constantly correcting Christi's immature behavior. One of her books labeled this type of parenting as doling out "emotional spankings." There must be a better way. The two of them were on a hamster wheel and somehow, she had to get off. Christi no doubt was feeling rejected and unloved but was too young to articulate it. But she was perceptive, as Pirsig put it, on the pre-intellectual level.

Besides books, Linda had always been drawn to the arts. Prior to Christi, she had enjoyed going to art museums and attending an occasional symphony concert. She went with women friends since these pursuits held no interest for Larry. They no longer shared night events like evening TV, occasional dramatic productions or movies on the weekends. These became something they used to do. He was a beach and tennis person and wanted her to be like the wives of his colleagues, so she filled her wardrobe with swimming suits and beach towels, white shorts and tennis outfits. She even learned how to play a decent game.

During those early years before becoming a mother, Linda had enjoyed a successful teaching career, but all the while she had dreamed of the time when she could create a comfortable, beautiful home for her husband and any children that might come their way. She had hoped that Larry would be a cooperative helpmate, to the extent his work allowed. She admired, and yes, envied, some of her friends whose husbands were more helpful. Not that she expected him to spend all his off-time doing household chores, but couldn't he change a light bulb once in a while without blowing up?

She recognized with growing discomfort that she had walked into as dysfunctional a situation as her own family, minus the economic struggles caused by her father's flitting from venture to venture. She had chosen financial stability over all else, naively believing that all other discordant personality traits would cure themselves. But instead, she found herself as isolated, lonely and depressed as she had been during her growing-up years.

Where was the gregarious Larry she had met and admired? Or, was she, as Larry accused her, the source of the problem? Part of the answer lay in his heavy drinking. Coming from an alcohol-free family, she did not recognize that she was witnessing an insidious march toward alcoholism. She figured that the nightcaps were his way to relax after a hard day at work. But she began to be suspicious that there might be more drinking than she observed at home or on weekends at the tennis club, where, between sets, he would order two or three margaritas followed by a tuaca liqueur, which he took straight or on the rocks. He brushed her off when she mentioned it. She cared little for the taste of liquor herself, could take it or leave it. It was the lifestyle in Southern California in the 1970s, he said, clearly becoming impatient with her. He would push her to experiment with drinks, chiding her that she had wanted to escape her provincial, overly moralistic background. Get used to it, he'd say.

He tried to change her. He wanted her to be tan and thin and to dye her hair blonde. He became obsessed with image, telling her how the wife of a successful business executive should look. She watched her weight but could not bring herself to buy a bottle of peroxide. With effort, she might transform herself into what he wanted, a tennis-playing, tanned version of his ideal mate. Well, not the tan, because her fair skin only burned.

She begged off doing beach time in the morning and early afternoon, explaining that her red-head's complexion with ultra-fair skin burned within minutes. Clearly, he was disappointed. Her compromise was to join him later in the afternoon. She'd fix a picnic supper and dutifully appear with a wicker basket filled with napkins, ham sandwiches, apples, cookies and a bottle of wine. Lemonade or canned soft drinks, of course, for Christi. But he continued to press for remaking herself in his desired image. Failure washed over her like the ocean waves pounding in from the Pacific where he and Christi cavorted, oblivious to Linda's submerged misery. Flotsam arrived with the waves, depositing sticks and crabs and shells upon the beach.

She approached Larry a number of times with the idea of talking about how they might communicate better. Finding time was not easy. Their meals together were becoming as rare as snow in Southern California. Efforts at establishing rapport ended up as another dinner disaster. Once when she pushed too far, he slapped her. Twice he encircled her throat with his hands but stopped himself before going too far. Then it was as if nothing had happened, and he became cheerful again. She hid the problem, did not discuss it with anyone. Instead, she began to harbor a deep apprehension that Larry might harm her. That was motivation enough to keep things calm on the surface.

An incident happened during their engagement period, one which should have waved a red flag. They were standing in her backyard talking about how they would be getting ready for their wedding ceremony in one month, just after Thanksgiving. Indian summer lingers in the Southwest, and the sycamore leaves, still green, murmured in the breeze. She was excited about the coming events, especially the anticipated move away from her parents.

He had turned to look at her, and Linda thought she saw in his eyes the same burning desire that throbbed within her breast. Their engagement had already been over a year, and they were excited to begin living their lives together. Linda was sure that he was equally enthralled by this delicious moment when they stood on the precipice of a new life that promised fulfillment and joy. She held Larry's hand and thought that he too was basking in the golden glow of their love on that bright October day.

Unexpectedly, Larry asked abruptly if she would write a paper for him, one due for one of his history classes. He claimed that he was too busy trying to work after school at the post office and help plan their wedding and do his duties as president of his business fraternity. It was as if an evil thing had intruded into their companionship. Something had shattered the mood that she thought was so romantic.

Linda was appalled at the request. Cheating was something she would never do. She declined as gracefully as possible, but he became furious, suddenly encircling his hands around her throat until she was able to peel him off. In shock, she turned and walked away from him, into her house. From her bedroom window, which faced the street, she heard him gun the motor of his car. She caught a glimpse of the gold Ford convertible roaring off.

❦

Looking back and realizing who she was, she could recognize a resemblance in the life she was living now to unpleasant experiences in her childhood. In some ways, she was repeating her efforts to be the perfect daughter to please her mother and gain her father's attention. Only she had transferred those patterns now as wife and mother. Her spirits sagged, along with her confidence that she would be a good mother to Christi and a proper wife to Larry. She began to weep during the day, drying her tears by mid-afternoon when she walked down the hill from their home to meet Christi at the school bus. Lumpy dark pockets appeared under her eyes. Though still in her mid thirties, she saw that she was sliding closer to middle age.

Still, she kept up appearances, continuing her volunteer work at Christi's school and with several organizations related to Larry's business. In the evening, she fed Christi and herself and heated up a plate for Larry when he returned late. Depression seeped into her whole being, and though she tried, she could not turn it away. The steak dinner had been a demarcation line in their relationship. One evening, without any particular trigger, she burst into tears, surprising Larry, who stared at her blankly.

Obviously puzzled, he snapped, "You're manufacturing crises that don't exist. You read too many books, too much women's lib, shit like that. That isn't the real world. All you want are fairy tales and dancing dolls. I live in the real world, and you don't appreciate how hard that is."

She tried to mollify him, to tell him she did value his ability to support the family. Then she approached him with an idea gathering strength in her mind, that of going to graduate school or getting a job since Christi was older, claiming that she needed to reclaim some identity apart from home and family.

"That's ridiculous," he answered. "Your income is secondary and most of it would go to taxes. If you're so impatient to go back to work, I'll set you up in business, say a travel agency, and we can write off all sorts of things."

Linda recoiled at that suggestion. "But I'm not interested in that," she said. "I want to do something fulfilling."

"Then why don't you join some organizations that will get clients for me?" Linda's dizzy spells must have started about that time.

◈

Establishing long-lasting friendships had not been easy. They had moved six times in seven years so that Larry could climb the corporate ladder. But now that they were settled in one place, Linda wanted more couple friendships. At one time, Larry had presented himself as an agreeable, cheerful, engaging dinner partner. They entertained his business associates, of course. However, when Linda began to invite former teaching colleagues and their spouses, Larry showed signs of discomfort. She observed that he was cheerful only among those whom he could impress or dominate.

He demeaned her academic acquaintances, remarking, "I don't intend to associate with losers. Anyone not working in the private sector is taking welfare." Linda pointed out that it was that "welfare" job in the public schools that had gotten them on their feet financially while he was gaining experience as an underpaid trainee in a large corporation. She had not meant this comment as a power play, but she should have realized that he would feel diminished, taking her remarks badly.

She thought about her father, how he bored people with his stories about himself, and how Larry did the same thing in front of her friends, although her father was not as inclined to inflate his accomplishments. Her mother had told her of times of bridge playing with other couples, only to endure the embarrassment of hearing her husband talk endlessly about himself, prompting their social contacts to drift away. Now it was possible to feel some compassion for her mother.

For years, Linda endured Larry's denigrating remarks in the privacy of their home. But later they took wing as verbal floggings in front of their friends. Once they invited Dwight and Marilyn to share a casual dinner at the end of the week. Someone brought up the Vietnam War, how useless it was, how tragic, and how the government had continuously lied about the rationale for our presence there.

A public storm of invective spewed forth from Larry's mouth – angry, opinionated, venomous words. "The only way to show those people is to bomb them back to the Stone Age."

"Maybe we should listen to some of these claims," Linda said, mortified at his outburst.

Linda remembered her father's rants in the 1950s about the McCarthy hearings, how many Communists were all around us and how McCarthy was the savior that called them out. The flashback was all too real.

Scowling and pointing his finger at her, Larry said angrily, "*You* made the mistake of inviting them over on a Friday night, now *you* listen!"

Marilyn asked for more coffee, attempting to snuff out the conversation and cover their embarrassment.

The public humiliations continued. Larry seemed to get pleasure out of degrading her in front of guests as if he were joking. She laughed along also, in public. When the subject of travel arose in conversation, he mentioned how poor her map reading skills were. He pantomimed turning a map every which way, eliciting gales of laughter. Without sounding too defensive, she joined in the merriment. She mentioned, smiling, that he was driving fast in traffic while she tried to figure out their way around an unfamiliar city. And wasn't this typical of clueless wives? In private, she seethed and asked him to stop.

Where had Larry's antagonism come from? And why was she the target? She was in touch with her own childhood bruises and bumps but wondered if there was something in his upbringing that she did not know about. He seemed to be happy and successful at work, so something else must be the trigger. What could it be?

❦

A group of women friends with whom Linda regularly met decided to have a dinner party that included spouses. On the way to the hosts' home, she gathered up the courage to ask him not to put her down or roar about politics. She mentioned that other people may have different political views.

As gently as she could, she said softly, "You know, people see things differently. We don't have to agree with them, but we can be polite."

Larry snorted and tossed his head arrogantly. "Well, they're all screwed up anyway. So why bother trying to talk sense to them?"

"Well, what's there to discuss when you close the door and say that everyone is wrong?" Linda retorted, sensing that no good things would come from this social event.

The hosts were cordial. Introductions and smiles set the stage for a convivial gathering. At first Larry socialized with everyone and mostly restrained himself until he drank a bit too much and starting bragging. First, he mentioned that he'd brought the first woman into Toastmasters. Then he mentioned how he had quit the Lutheran church because of the hypocrites who refused to admit a black family. He also announced that he'd been president of his local Lion's Club chapter, president of his insurance honorary designation society, and that his insurance firm was one of the top three in the city. The more he boasted, the more the dinner guests shifted in their seats. Linda cringed. She saw their eyes. He was repeating his sentences, beginning to slur words. He was not at all aware of how he was affecting others. They were bored and no doubt mortified for her. She sat stone-faced, helpless to stop the stream of braggadocio.

When it was time to leave, the husband of one of her friends refused to shake Larry's hand. No invitations to dinner parties ever came from that group again. Linda was not surprised, but crushed.

※

To get some handle on her crashing world, Linda had tried therapy. She deliberately chose a woman, thinking that this person would understand her marital concerns better than a male therapist. However, after the sessions had ended, she wondered whether Dr. Whitmore was in tune with feminine concerns. Linda's reading had made her aware of a wide variety of feminist writings, some from earlier centuries, others from popular books fueling a full-fledged women's consciousness movement, which was swirling around, questioning long-held notions of male superiority and the legitimacy (in men's eyes) of female submissiveness.

But Dr. Whitmore did not want to explore these angles. Instead, she expressed that Linda was overreacting to Larry's behavior because of her early rejection by her father. She did begin to see parallels – the self-blame that had infected her childhood had bubbled up to spill into her married life. But was there more to it than that? At first, she would return from these sessions more troubled than ever, reinforced in the belief that somehow she was the cause of the deteriorating relationship. But why, Linda thought between sessions, did Dr. Whitmore not suggest that Larry might be overreacting to something?

She had been too timid to bring up this question and confront Dr. Whitmore with it. Although she was just beginning to discover her own strength, she had not yet dropped all of the shackles that bound her. Later, she realized that she had viewed Dr. Whitmore as an authority figure whom she dared not question. She sometimes got angry, wondering if this all-powerful counselor understood her concerns at all. But had this been Dr. Whitmore's strategy all along – to get her client to transfer the latent anger at her father – and to a lesser extent her mother – over her childhood deprivations, and thus discharge some of it?

With time, Linda began to recognize that she had taken responsibility for each relationship's failure entirely on her own shoulders, instead of valuing herself as a person worthy of being treated fairly. To her credit, she protested more openly with Larry than she had with her father. With both, however, her fears of their reprisals limited the amount of dissent she dared utter.

Larry, seeing his wife falling apart emotionally, agreed to couple's counseling with Dr. Whitmore.

"I'll do whatever it takes for you to fix your problem," he said.

"My problem? I was hoping we might get some help on how to communicate better with each other," Linda replied.

Linda could hardly bear the arrogant smirk on Larry's face during these sessions. After two meetings, he refused to continue. He said that things were just fine and that he could not understand what all the fuss was about. It was entirely his wife's problem; she was exaggerating the entire situation. Linda noticed that he directed his comments directly to Dr. Whitmore, never involving her – Linda – in the conversation. Linda chimed in when she could, saying that she had hoped their marriage would be one of mutual support, not just her supporting all *his* needs. But it was clear that Larry was resistant to change, and Dr. Whitmore told Linda that if Larry did not want to engage in further sessions, there was little she could do to help.

It had taken her far too long to examine her belief that it was *her* duty to do all the changing and adaptation. Duty drove her, along with her strong belief that loyalty was all-important, as had been the case with her mother. But Linda was about to take a risk that her mother refused to consider. Once she was able to put ambivalence behind her, Linda's resolve was unyielding. Exhilaration motivated her, side by side with relief.

Making the decision to leave took time. She would come to the edge, then back away. But finally, she knew she had to sever the ties. She already had learned enough about money matters by taking over the family finances, and she knew she would have to go back to work. Additionally, she consulted a female lawyer to get a handle on what her economic prospects might be. What she learned gave her additional confidence.

❧

The in-laws were coming to visit – Larry's widowed mother, his brother and wife along with their two-year-old son. Linda did most of the preparations. The yard was overgrown, and she welcomed the outdoor work. Digging in the yard, clearing away weeds helped her brush away her depression, temporarily.

A lichen commonly known as "witch's hair" grew profusely over the bougainvillea covering a fence sloping down the driveway. By now, it had taken over, covering the scarlet blossoms with a sickly saffron-colored web resembling tangled straw. It was not a simple job to remove it. The bougainvillea was thorny; even her thick gardening gloves sometimes got pierced. She started pulling away swaths of the stuff when she spied on an embankment of ice plant over the fence a ball of fur. Stepping closer, she discovered an injured owl, tan-tipped and blue-feathered, its wing torn enough to prevent flying and its foot mangled. It emerged from a curled ball and hopped about, hiding among the boulders, frightened, shy, unable to defend itself. Linda ran into the house and phoned the animal control department. When they arrived, Linda was relieved to hear that they would deliver the owl immediately to a veterinarian.

Linda could not erase the image of the bird from her mind. It began to take on more significance than the event normally would have warranted. She had learned that some Native American cultures associated owls with death. Here she was, living in the midst of a dying marriage. But weren't owls also associated with wisdom? Athena, goddess of wisdom in Greek mythology, was at times portrayed with an owl on her shoulder. She knew that she had been unwise to marry Larry, but now she wanted to make better choices. Was this knowledge the beginning of wisdom, or simply a dream of escape? Would wisdom suddenly drop like a golden mantle over her confused psyche, or would it develop over time much as the owl grew its feathers?

One night she dreamed that a woman tried to leave a room to go somewhere to comfort a screaming child, but the woman couldn't get out because the door was stuck. There were boards on it with sticks and nails coming out from it. The woman screamed, "I can't get out of here!" From somewhere came another scream, "Turn on the light!" She awoke wondering if the dream was trying to tell her that the answers may be right there, inside, as accessible as a light switch.

※

When his family arrived, Larry switched his demeanor back to charming. He bustled around helping set the table, doing barbecue duty on the deck. He would show them what a good husband and father he was. Christi reveled in the extra attention and banished whining for the time being.

But then the fire erupted. Larry had dumped the coals from the grill into a plastic bag and then into a trash can. Suddenly the garage was ablaze. Horrified, they could see the flames below them as they stood on the deck. Larry started ordering everyone around, acting as if it was everyone's fault but his. Even his worshiping brother began to see a side of him he didn't know existed. The fire department responded readily. Quick work and reliant hoses did the trick. There was no spread to other parts of the dwelling. Just a little electrical damage. More easily fixed than marriages turned to ashes.

Panicked at the thought of leaving Larry, yet knowing that the cut had to come, she thought distractedly, "Now which one of us will get Dudley?"

Chapter Nine
A World Shattered

January, 1977

"Just take me to an orphanage and let me die! I'll never see Daddy again, and I won't have a Grandma anymore," she screamed. "I hate you!" Larry was present for the breaking of the news, but she directed all her anger toward her mother. For Christi, the blonde, blue-eyed darling of her parents, the world had just blown up.

Christi's initial response to the forthcoming divorce was not a surprise. In fact, Linda had anticipated such an eruption. She had dreaded the aftermath of the announcement for weeks, but there was no escape. The time had come to tell her.

Larry had agreed to let them stay until details could be worked out for the move out of their home. Linda was determined to make a new start, but not in Southern California. After much pondering, she decided to return to her childhood home in New Mexico, where she still had friends, and the cost of living was reasonable.

It would be several weeks before she and Christi could depart. Linda had been vague about the timing of the move, feeling that Christi needed some time to absorb the major shock before presenting the fact that she would be leaving her friends and school, Brownie meetings and birthday parties, and thrust into a foreign world.

Up to now, her world had been all too perfect with never a thought that it could crack wide open. Larry's mother sent dollar bills on holiday occasions, and Christi begged her father to make frequent treks to the toy store. At different points in her short life, she owned various small pets – hamsters, guinea pigs and bunnies. She also cared for a silent menagerie of stuffed poodles, alligators and bears. Hers had been a fairytale existence, safe from things that hurt or crush or smash.

But now, the pieces splintered in all directions, and in the days that followed, so did Christi. As she struggled to cope with this major shift, a number of new Christis emerged. There was wrathful Christi, who flung herself dramatically on the russet wool carpet, regressing into a toddler's temper tantrum. Or, angelic Christi would emerge, meticulously arranging a normally helter-skelter room.

Linda met grown-up Christi who advised her logically, "I think you and Daddy *should* get a divorce. I hate to see people unhappy." But a puzzled Christi wandered aimlessly through the house asking, "Why? Why?"

Determined Christi told Linda firmly, "I can take it. I can adjust." But depressed Christi spoke alarmingly, "I'm going to find an accident to make me die."

Just before the announcement, Linda presented Christi with her favorite childhood doll.

"This was Mommy's doll. I used to call her Sara. But you can name her yourself," Linda said, pleased to be passing along a special childhood treasure, hoping it would give Christi something to cling to after the shock was delivered. Christi beamed, "Oh thank you, Mommy! I'll call her Sara, too."

But that was before Christi knew. Now, that once-glowing face was contorted, signaling a coming furious storm. Sara was about to be delivered into safekeeping.

"Here, Mommy, you put Sara on a shelf. I just don't know what I might do to her. Sometimes, I want to *kill* her!" Sara's head was molded of breakable material, which more than once had been patched and painted at the doll hospital. Linda envisioned a fractured skull and agreed at once.

Together, they wrapped the doll in one of Christi's saved baby blankets and toted her off to a spare bedroom where Sara could take up residence in a cedar chest. But they agreed to leave the tiny doll crib beside Christi's bed just in case she should want Sara's company again, when she felt that she could manage those previously uncontrollable episodes. Christi showed an amazing self-perception of her potential to explode. Have patience, Linda told herself; that awareness is a good sign.

In the quiet but submerged turbulence that marked the days before the final move, Linda sometimes would find a piece of toast and a glass of juice waiting for her at the breakfast table – Christi's offerings, Linda suspected, to insure on-going protection.

Without being asked, Christi took the family dog for walks when she came home from school. Linda did not have to remind her to feed Thumper the bunny and clean his cage. In the late afternoons or on Saturdays, Christi embarked upon other projects. She organized the toys and games in her room. She dusted shelves adorned with the fluff of a stuffed animal's fur and scattered with grains of sand from a swimming suit carelessly flung about the room. She swept the sidewalks free of heaped leaves and asked if she could wash pots and pans not used for years. She worked feverishly, as if driven.

At night, though, Linda would awaken to Christi's shrieking, go to her room to rock her and soothe away the terrors of her disturbing nightmares. They were full of knives and scissors, things that cut or split or separate. In one, she related that someone got killed in a car wreck, and a woman had forced her, Christi, to look at the body. In another, a woman and child were in a boat that got upset. The child reached the boat, but the woman floated out to sea and disappeared in a whirlpool. Linda held her worries in check, convincing herself that since Christi was telling her about these wretched nightmares, there must be some trust left. Linda hoped that was the case.

Linda had procrastinated to avoid upsetting Christi's life. But after much soul-searching, she realized that "for the sake of the child" was an excuse to avoid coming to terms with the viability of her marriage. Although she believed in the ultimate wisdom of her decision, doubts tortured her. And Christi's fitful tossings served as a reminder of the terrible battles *she* was fighting. Nor were the struggles confined to the terrors of the dark; for Christi learned, cleverly, to mask her fears.

"Will I be your daughter even after you're divorced?" That one met with a rapid, affirmative response.

But Linda had no ready answers for such inquiries as, "Will Daddy come to visit?" Or, "If Daddy marries someone else and there are kids, will he still want me?" All she could do was say, "Christi, Mommy and Daddy both love you and always will."

"But why didn't you tell me sooner?" On the surface, to Christi, and to their friends, life moved along in normal fashion, for Linda had managed to hide the inner turmoil she had been experiencing for years.

One day came a remark that set Linda on her heels. She had explained to Christi that she and Larry would try to remain friends and not hate each other like so many other couples that separate. Although it took a while for Christi to ponder this idea, she finally blurted out, "Well, if you're such good friends, why are you breaking up your relationship?"

She said *relationship*? Seven-year-olds were smarter than those of her own generation, she thought. Linda decided it not wise to explain to her the bitter hurts, the lack of emotional support, the gradual distancing, the slow but inevitable breakdown leading to a crack in the bond, which, never repaired, had opened to an irreparable chasm.

Linda attempted an answer although she knew it was a weak response. "I don't expect you to understand this now, but perhaps you will, some day. I want you to bring your questions to me. You make me think." Linda tried to smile as she spoke. But this was not enough for Christi.

Gradually, Linda came up with superficial explanations to the interrogations that would not go away.

"Your father and I are very different. He thinks work is the most important thing in his life. He wants only to play tennis in his spare time. I would like us to spend weekend time as a family, doing a picnic in the park, going to a museum or a musical concert or seeing an art show. He has no interest in these sorts of the things. To have a loving family, we need to share a few things together. You know as well as I do that we don't go to the beach or on picnics together as we used to do." Linda knew she was stalling, wondering if she were saying too much or too little for Christi's mind to absorb.

In the beginning, Christi said, "Okay, I *think* I get it." Good, Linda heaved a sigh or relief. She was on the right track.

But no. Christi persisted in asking, "Why?" Same answers, different words. And then it came to her, that Christi wasn't really interested in reasons, but that she was hiding a terrible bit of knowledge in her still developing brain.

"I guess *I'm* the reason you're breaking up, right?"

Night terrors, hideous dreams…and now this. She had at last verbalized it, her terrible fears of being the cause of the breakup. It had been right in front of her, but Linda had missed it.

"No, Christi, you are in no way responsible. The problems your father and I are having started years before you were born. And we both feel it's better for you in the long run if we stop pretending."

For a long while after that, Christi stopped asking, "Why?" In fact, she startled Linda soon after this conversation with, "Mommy, I hope you get married again." Well, thought Linda, how nice. She wants me to be happy. And Christi persisted, clinging to this thought doggedly, "Mommy, please get married again."

Linda had learned that Christi's statements held hidden meanings, not always discerned. Not wishing to dampen her enthusiasm, but wanting to be honest, Linda replied, "I don't know whether there will be someone for me to marry again. It may take a long time. But if that should happen, you will be part of a new family, but also always have your own Dad."

Finally, the hidden perplexity burst open, and she shouted, "But I don't want you to marry someone else! If you can get un-married to Daddy, you can also get married to him. With a more subdued voice, she begged, "Will you *please* marry Daddy again?"

As difficult as it was to say, Linda replied, "No, Christi, that is not going to be possible."

Christi wrapped her fears around herself like a rope. Deep within, she was plotting how to knot the noose, toss the loop and corral her parents into becoming a familiar family of three once again.

Linda thought of how long it had taken her to come to the point of admitting that divorce was the appropriate route. She reflected on the years of immeasurable physical, mental and emotional energy she had expended in vacillation, in lack of resolution, in attempts to adapt and conform to Larry's expectations. The struggle had taken its toll in depression and anxiety. How, then, could she expect Christi to overcome her grief on short notice? Time, she kept reminding herself, it really takes time.

In those last days before the moving van appeared at the door, Linda took special care to spend extra time with Christi before bedtime, trying to rock away the anger, the hurt, the loss. The nightmares diminished but reared up occasionally. She continued her resistance to change, but Linda had to admire her stubbornness, the quality that would become her later strength. Linda knew that she was coping with her first real-world challenge, and she prayed that in the long run it would benefit, rather than cripple, her character.

Linda was learning to sniff out what lay behind that innocent mask of too much helpfulness, to perceive the patterns she had missed at first. In her darker moments, as the time to leave grew closer, she could imagine Christi smashing Sara's head again and again in uncontrollable rage, then cuddling the doll tenderly. Wave after wave of contradictory emotions hit her. She was finding her baby once again but also seeing her all grown up and wise.

"We're going on a long trip, Christi. And we'll be living in a place very different from the Pacific Coast. It's an adventure. And Granddaddy wants to go with us, to help with the driving. Then he'll go back to California by himself. You'll be making new friends and going to a different school. I know you are going to do just fine. And Daddy and I will make sure you get to see him."

There, the news was out. Christi looked askance at her mother but did not appear to be stunned. With a perspicacity that Linda had overlooked, Christi already knew. Or she had dissembled to protect herself.

Christi snuggled in her mother's arms, looked into her face with pleading, sad but knowing eyes and asked, "Since we're moving away, can Thumper and Dudley go with us? And Sara? What will we see along the way?"

Linda returned her look, not with fear but with a pained smile. "Lots of desert, Christi. Lots and lots of desert."

Chapter Ten
Journey East

"...if I had to choose one plant to express the spirit of the Sonoran Desert – one which combines oddness of form and habit with the courage to flourish under seemingly impossible conditions, and which combines also the defensive fierceness of thorns with the spectacular, unexpected beauty of brilliant flowers – I think I should choose the ocotillo."
—Joseph Wood Krutch, *The Desert Year*

April, 1977

"There's a sign to Yuma. 13 miles. You promised we'd stop for ice cream in Yuma, Granddaddy," pleaded Christi. "This drive's so bor – Look, Mommy, there's a roadrunner."

"Sorry, Christi, I missed it. We're going so fast." Not fast enough to get through this God-forsaken desert, Linda thought. Even if an Arizona policeman clocking their speed might pull them over, they'd be closer to the end of this desolate waste of earth. Worth the fine, maybe.

Cactus, nothing but cactus, for miles. With her father at the wheel driving the white Toyota Corolla station wagon at ninety miles per hour, she felt as if they were cooped in a spaceship hurtling across another planet, breaking the time barrier throughout a surreal adventure. All earthly time vanished. She had the sensation of a concurrent ability to look backward at all she had been and had become and forward to what might lie ahead, as inscrutable as that might be. All in this white capsule streaking eastward to an unknown destiny.

Linda sat with Christi in the back seat, trying to occupy her daughter with board checkers, puzzles and books. Dudley the dachshund lay next to them, listless and lethargic. With her father at the wheel, Linda imagined that an alien with gnarled hands was driving them with abandon across miles of asphalt surrounded by cactus. Until they could switch driving duties at the next stop, he was in charge of their fate.

The ocotillos were in bloom. There must have been spring rains, welcome since the majority of the desert moisture happened in July during the monsoon season. Brilliant blossoms burst like flames at the top of spiky gray-green sticks. Tentacles, they look like tentacles, reaching for something. She was thankful for the ocotillos. Their blossoms relieved the tans and grays and muddy greens they had seen since leaving the California seacoast and dropping over the mountains to the desert floor.

Scooting forward on the smoothly grained blue vinyl, Linda wedged her fingers into an open space between the front headrest and the top of the front seat. She wanted her voice to be heard above the whooshing produced in the car as they flew over the highway pavement.

"I suppose we could take a break, Daddy. We left the Coast nearly five hours ago. Seven-year-olds get tired of checkers pretty fast. Maybe we could find a rest stop even before we get to Yuma."

Still perched on the edge of her seat, Linda glanced into the rear view mirror, where she caught a flash of annoyance in her father's eyes. Still, she knew he would stop for Christi, but not for her when she was seven.

"Well, if you can wait for a few more miles, I suppose we could stop for some gas in Yuma. Maybe find a Dairy Queen," he said, some of his words getting muffled in the droning sound inside their veritable flying machine.

Soaring away, she was definitely doing that. Once Linda announced her decision to dissolve the marriage and move back to New Mexico where she had grown up, Larry had spoken angrily, "Ok, just take the kid, the bunny and the dog, and go – I don't give a rat's ass about what you do. It's over!"

She realized in retrospect that the coarse language, which she hated, had been escalating for several years now, and that she had tolerated it without saying anything to him about it. She had tried to pick her battles. They were just words, she told herself. Words can't hurt, she told herself, just as the childhood jingle said. But they had grated around the edges, affecting her attitude toward him, yet she had submerged her displeasure, knowing that he would chide her for being too uptight, too straight-laced. That last sentence, though, signaled what she was forced to face: what those eighteen years had meant – or not meant – to him.

༺༻

The big surprise was that her father offered to help with the driving. He told her that he had written, without informing her beforehand, a motel in Tucson – their half-way point – booking two rooms, telling her about these arrangements after the fact. Linda tried not to ascribe cynical motives to her father but nevertheless had wondered if he might be grasping at yet another opportunity to go on the road. Or maybe he just wanted some time with Christi, a grandfather's delight. Age had not diminished his restlessness. He had just passed his seventy-ninth birthday, but reminded Linda of a young pup tugging on its leash, begging for freedom to run the path.

She had been on only one other trip with him. It happened during the summer just after her high school graduation. Her father had startled her with proposing that they journey, just the two of them, out to the West Coast. They could stay with one of Linda's aunts, her father's sister, so the trip would be affordable. That was important. Money was hard to come by.

Maybe that was the consolation prize for his missing her graduation ceremony. The sting of that was still festering, competing for attention as they drove west through the orange groves of Arizona. But it diminished once she gasped at her first view of the Pacific Ocean.

He was jovial on that trip, pleased to be traveling once again, showing her sights in the Los Angeles area, taking her to Catalina Island where he treated her to a ride on a glass-bottomed boat. Linda had stared in wonder at the plethora of sea life wriggling beneath her, the flashing silvery scales slithering and disappearing before her eyes, just as her childhood was swimming out of sight before the cognizance of the lost years had sunk in.

Now, Linda hoped that, by offering to be the chauffeur, her father was trying to make up for all the years of negligence while she was growing up. Perhaps he was trying to tell her without speaking it that he understood why she was leaving Larry. He was aware that she knew about his two-year disastrous marriage prior to meeting her mother, but never had he mentioned it to her.

"You know, he loves you very much," he had said to her at the start of their trip. "You can win him back." But, true to form, her father neither asked her whether she wanted to "win him back" nor why she was leaving. Then suspicion set in, and Linda also wondered if he had undertaken the journey in hopes of persuading her to stay with Larry. Her father hadn't a clue. He thought of love in terms of what he felt for Linda's mother, which was genuine and real. Linda was certain that Larry loved no one but himself.

She had tried to save her marriage, but Larry also bore some responsibility as his drinking problem became worse. There had been frightening times when she thought her husband would harm her. She wondered what her father might think if he knew that Larry took several drinks per evening and did martini lunches with clients besides. There were matters that she simply could not share with her father.

The air conditioner whirred, pumping cool air throughout the car. Linda was grateful for it. Otherwise, she could scarcely endure this trip to New Mexico with Christi grumbling in the heat and her father droning on about "those durn fool liberal politicians" and that we should have done more bombing in Vietnam to "get rid of those Communists" and "that's how we lost the war" because "Am-ur-ica has lost its moral compass."

"Are we almost there, Mommy?" Christi whined. She was wiggling again after assembling a horse puzzle on her lap board. "I can't wait to get my ice cream."

"Let's play the cloud game," Linda suggested. "I see a cloud that looks like a…" Linda looked at Christi hopefully.

"Dragon!" Christi shrieked. Then, "Look, over there – it's a bunny, just like Thumper! And there's a long one…a dachshund, just like Dudley! See those little clouds hanging down? Just like Dudley's short legs."

"Oh," she said, "Thumper died. I wanted to bring him along on this trip." Christi threw her head back with a jolt and gave another moan, perhaps a veiled accusation. Linda sighed. Christi had wanted to keep the bunny inside, but her parents had insisted it would be fine in its cage in the backyard. They had failed to account for the cleverness of raccoons that had managed to remove the hasp on the cage.

Christi turned away from the window and took up her sketch pad. Apparently, that was the end of the cloud game. Patience, patience. Linda restrained herself from being cross with her daughter. "Soon, Christi, soon," she replied.

The car streaked eastward, a lone moving object on the desert horizon. From the cool cocoon of the automobile, Linda surveyed the terrain. Piercing blue, that's what the sky was, with elusive strands of clouds moving about, joining and separating, reminding her of the back and forth uncertainty that preceded her departure. The stark landscape – parched earth, caked rivulets, and giant saguaros with their strange, distorted shapes – all served as a significant reminder of her internal desert.

When Linda told her daughter about the saguaros, Christi's eyes widened, hearing that woodpeckers made their homes in those giant cacti, and that sometimes, if you walked on the desert floor and stayed really quiet, you could hear them pecking.

※

Dry, dry, how could anything live where it's so dry, Linda thought. She was becoming increasing uncomfortable with what lay ahead. In the distance loomed a mountain range. Those purple, rugged peaks made her shudder, yet they were beautiful in their barrenness. At every turn of the highway, they changed character as soft shadows gathered in their crevices, then separated and diffused.

Billboard ads announced that they were approaching Yuma. "There's one, Granddaddy, a Dairy Queen! Please turn around!" Christi was bouncing, scattering puzzle pieces everywhere. Once Christi got something on her mind it was hard to divert her. Linda wanted to scream. No sounds emerged from her throat, however.

"There will be another one. Yuma can be hot even at this time of year. There'll be lots of ice cream places," her grandfather said. "I'll be slowing down soon, you'll see. Maybe you'll want a hamburger, too."

"No, Granddaddy, just an ice cream sundae," Christi said, a bit sulkily. "With lots of whipped cream and a cherry on top," she added.

The station wagon slid easily into the parking lot of a clean-looking diner. It was a Big Boy restaurant. Outside, a model of an overgrown young boy was balancing a huge hamburger on his palm. The figure dominated the setting in front of the restaurant. Had the outside temperature been more moderate, Linda could imagine Christi trying to climb up to the fat boy's prodigious waist. She felt dizzy. All she wanted was a glass of iced tea.

Her father ordered coffee, and they sipped their refreshments silently while Linda marveled how Christi could devour the sundae. When it was three-quarters gone, Christi began to pout. "I want another cherry," she said. "They look like my marbles, like the ones Daddy and I used to play. Mommy, can I play marbles when we get there?" Marbles reminded Linda of her childhood rolling, rolling away into adulthood and now rolling again into an indefinite somewhere.

She squeezed another lemon wedge and let it fall into her tea glass with a plop. The thought of whipping cream and another maraschino cherry made her stomach churn.

They returned to the car, and once through town, they passed back into the desert open spaces. This time, Linda sat in front beside her father. Christi, thankfully, was in the back drawing pictures of roadrunners. She adjusted the headrest and relaxed her neck. She hadn't intended to sleep, just rest for a while. Dreams, nightmares tumbled about in her head.

Christi's legs pumped like pistons. Chasing a roadrunner. Someone flew after her making the desert dust billow. Gasping, choking, heaving, catching Christi, looking at her face – her own face. Pulling away from Larry, Christi screaming...running on the desert, losing Christi, finding her behind a saguaro, Christi laughing, teasing, dashing behind ocotillos just missing their spiky thorns...Larry calling them back...Christi and the Big Boy... Christi as tall as his waist, grown to be a young woman...Christi chasing another roadrunner...No, Christi, stop...you'll run forever...marbles rolling on the desert...you'll have to eat your ice cream in the desert...Don't you hear the woodpecker? Christi stopping, listening...tapping...then puddles of melted ice cream, water...mirrors, mirages, her own face looking into all of them...

"Nothing but static on the radio." Her father's voice caused her to jerk her head abruptly to the perpendicular.

"Mommy, look at my roadrunner. I drew it while you were asleep."

"That's great, Christi." Linda turned her head toward the backseat where Christi was working expertly with butcher paper and crayons. "You're a good little artist," she mumbled sleepily.

"Granddaddy, when will we be in Tucson? What's in the Desert Museum? You said you might take me there. And that painter's house, the one with all the paintings of Indian children. Will you, Granddaddy? Please?"

"Ted DeGrazia," Linda filled in. We saw some of his paintings in the art museum. You have a good memory!"

"We'll see, Christi. Linda, you were out for quite a while. How about a rest stop? I think the car should cool down." For once, her father was willing to pace himself. "Then it will be only a couple more hours to Tucson." She was fully conscious now and welcomed her father's suggestion. She was aching to escape from the car. Her father must have seen the rest stop sign, because suddenly the tires bounced off the pavement onto a narrow gravel path leading to an area with a few picnic tables and restroom facilities.

"I'll get Dudley some water in his dish," her father offered. "If you like, I'll walk him around a bit."

Grateful for the offer, she nodded at him what she hoped he would take as a silent thank you. She had wanted desperately to take a walk alone, but she could hardly leave Christi, or Dudley for that matter, behind.

Taking Christi by the hand, Linda headed for the path she spied just beyond the farthest picnic table. The air was exceptionally warm for mid-April, maybe the high 80s. Hot and dry, but pleasant. Like L.A. when the hot east winds blow in and banish the smog. Maybe I could live once again in a New Mexico desert town, she thought. She wasn't so sure, though, about Christi. All she has known are trips to the beach, walks in wooded canyon parks and living her life in a home on the hillside with a backyard swimming pool. How much would she miss the father who indulged her with a surplus of toys? How difficult would the adjustment be from affluence to modest means? And having only one parent? Had her actions produced another kind of desert for Christi?

The ocotillo blossoms looked like flames ready to burn up the dry sage and rabbit bush. Those tentacles – they seemed to be searching, as she was, for the drift of the desert wind, for some kind of direction, just as she was. Surveying the desert scene from the walking path, she spied paper-thin wisps marked with geometric patterns lying scattered about the desert floor. Left-behind snake skins. Now she was shedding an old skin, that of a corporate wife, to venture into some kind of new form. The thought both terrified and thrilled her.

Christi pulled free after warnings to stay strictly on the path. Moving slowly, observing closely, Linda thought about how much of the desert detail she'd missed as the Corolla raced through this vast expanse. The walking path was narrow, and an unwelcome cactus thorn caught the leg of her pants. She turned quickly, only to hear and feel the rip. She looked down. The offending plant was a barrel cactus. Full of thorns, yes, but also covered with beautiful yellow flowers. She had never realized how gorgeous desert blooms could be. Several buds were just waiting to open. No wonder the cacti were so fat, storing up all that water. So isolated, yet surviving in their weird, grotesque forms. Would she find herself adjusting to new ways, just like the cacti, in a desert of her own making?

Sounds…a jay squawking, tires singing on the highway, insects whirring in the dry crackling air, a dull tapping, a buzz, a rattle. A rattle!…Her heart pounded and her stomach went cold, right in all that heat. She'd forgotten to warn Christi about snakes. Except for the cactus, the desert had seemed so sterile, so harmless.

Christi now was ahead down the path, looking carefully but not touching a cactus bloom. "Christi, time to go!" she yelled. Linda didn't want to frighten her, but she ran forward and grabbed Christi's hand. She whirled around and with a stunned Christi in tow, began racing toward the car. She ran as if the car were a mile away, yet in reality they had wandered only a few yards. She hadn't seen the snake, and chances were it wasn't even close. They are more afraid of us than we are of them, she had once learned from a forest ranger. Still, she shuddered, irrationally panicked over the unseen, rather than the visible.

"We're in good shape," her father announced, oblivious as always to what had just happened along the path. "I really didn't expect the radiator to overheat, not until it's really hot outside, 110 or so." He loosened the prop and slammed down the hood.

"Daddy," Linda said, "I want to drive. You need a rest. No reason why I shouldn't. I heard a rattler on my walk. Driving will give me a chance to get that off my mind." She knew she'd be in for the usual protests but decided to stand firm.

"Christi would really enjoy having you in the back seat. Couldn't you do a puzzle with her or something? She'd like that."

He nodded and walked around to the passenger side. Then he paused and looked over at her, as if he had been holding back his thoughts until what he perceived to be the right time, and spoke. "Now I'm not to going to ask you about your decision. But I will say this. That man loved you. Maybe you should think all this over."

Her father would never understand if she explained how she had tortured herself about making the decision to leave. She could not share all the parts of the story. She had made a decision, for good or ill, and she wasn't turning back.

Now she was in the driver's seat. Though she wanted to be out of the desert, she chose to cruise at a cautious sixty-five, more wary than her father of some policeman lurking behind a sand hill. Billboards began obscuring the cactus as they neared Tucson.

The walk in the desert had shaken her soul. The ocotillo with its waving arms, reaching out for something, and the woodpecker in the saguaro – those spoke to her. But with the sound of the rattler, she wondered if danger lay ahead for her, and maybe for Christi, too. She had not made the decision to sever her marital bonds without thought and foresight, but she was forced to admit that a certain amount of denial and magical thinking had accompanied her along the way.

"Can we go swimming, Mommy?" Christy asked.

"I expect so;" she replied, hiding her old fear of the water, but knowing how good the pool would feel after the long drive.

As she pushed down on the accelerator, she noticed the clouds gathering over the mountains and wondered if the weather might be changing. At the edge of town, they found the modest but comfortable looking motel that her father had booked. He had made sure the establishment would accept pets for one night. He took one room while she and Christi shared another.

Dudley was content after Christi dished out a bowl of Kibbles 'n Bits for him. Quickly unloading their suitcases, they located their swimsuits, changed and grabbed terry robes provided by the motel. They were about to leave when her father's voice came through after a tap on the door.

"Looks like a thunderstorm coming. Not too good of an idea to go in the water when there's lightning close." Echoes of her childhood. You can't go tobogganing because you might fall off and hurt your back. You can't ride a horse because your mother fell off once and sustained a concussion. You can't ski, you can't ride the roller coaster at the fair, you can't…Motivated by an overabundance of caution, her parents saw to it that she had lost out on many childhood pleasures. This time, she wasn't going to let a few ominous clouds keep her out of that pool.

"It's all right, Daddy, we'll watch carefully. Christi and I will get out if we see lightning. Just go have a cool drink."

Once he was gone, she and Christi trudged down a long corridor to the outside door leading to the pool area. Only a few sunbathers and swimmers were in sight.

The water rippled with puddles of light softened by the late afternoon sun. Christi was already swimming, arms and legs in perfect coordination, as Linda stood poised at the edge of the pool. Then she plunged deep, deep into the cool cavern. Liquid space enclosed her. Rising to the surface, she popped her head up, smoothing strands of wet hair back from her face. Close by she saw Christi, face upturned in a back float, beaming.

The sky darkened and a mugginess descended on the desert. Linda saw a streak across the sky, then another flash, and from the mountains came an ominous rumble. Dark balls of clouds – thunderheads – were roiling, moving toward them. They would have to retreat, and she called out to Christi, "One more, and then we go in."

She took another breath, and they both dived down again, wiggling like fish. By the time she bobbed to the surface, Christi's lithe frame had glided underwater to the opposite end of the pool where she emerged, clambering onto the concrete edge.

"Ooo, Mommy, rain!" Christi's voice skimmed the surface of the pool, reaching Linda's ears just in time.

Huge plunks of water began clicking in the pool. Treading water, Linda curled her tongue and exposed it to the sky, catching drops that slid ever so easily down her throat.

Part Three

I believe that one can never leave home. I believe that one carries the shadows, the dreams, the fears and the dragons of home under one's skin, at the extreme corners of one's eyes and possibly in the gristle of the earlobe.

—Maya Angelou, Letter to My Daughter

People give pain, are callous and insensitive, empty and cruel...but place heals the hurt, soothes the outrage, fills the terrible vacuum that these human beings make.
—Eudora Welty, *The Eye of the Story: Selected Essays and Reviews*

Chapter Eleven
Going Home

Three Years Later – 1980

With the journey east behind her, Linda embarked on a graduate program in education, one from which Larry had dissuaded her. The scariness of creating a new life had faded; each day brought new surprises and, remarkably, joy. By some miracle undeserved, she felt, she found true love with a soul mate – a gentle, thoughtful, affectionate man, sensitive to feelings and wise in so many ways. She and Matthew had known each other as friends years before at the university. Once they embarked on the commitment to a marriage and blending their families, they affiliated with a religious community dedicated to openness and social service. With the passing years came new inner strength, less mourning for what was missed in childhood, and more gratitude for her present life.

Christi's life had settled down, too, with new friends, soccer games, movies and a stepfather who was kind and compassionate, interested and involved in both her school and extra-curricular activities, unlike the dad left back in California who invited her to visit only once a year for one week. For Christi, the transition from an indulgent father to a sensible stepparent who lay down appropriate boundaries was not easy; but with time, parts of her former existence and the trauma of separation began to slip away.

By this time, Linda's parents had moved back to New Mexico also, having become disillusioned with California smog, traffic and crowds. Her mother had never wanted to move to California in the first place; but, as she had all her life, she gave into her husband's preferences against her better judgment. They had sold their comfortable home in Albuquerque and moved, finding housing about five miles from where Linda and Larry lived. But now, age had caught up with them, and they spent most of their time dealing with their many food sensitivities and coping with increasing infirmities. It was time to go home.

When Christi was ten, she began to plead with Linda. "Can you take me to the place where you grew up? I want to see the mud house where you used to live." She was beginning to know the difference between the here and now and what happened before she was born.

"Well, that can't be. It's gone by now, I'm sure. And it's called *adobe*, Christi."

Linda was reluctant to return to the small town of her childhood. She had no wish to revive memories long since buried in that dusty place. But Christi's begging became incessant, so finally Linda agreed, surprising herself at the magnetic pull of the idea.

She chose a day in May for the trip. Cruising along the interstate was a breeze now that commuters no longer were obligated to take the roads billowing with dust that wound through the Indian pueblo and village. As she sped along, she told an incredulous Christi about the sights and scents of her childhood.

Years ago, that was the only route between the little town where she lived with her family, and the more prosperous city to the north where one could purchase items not carried in local mercantile establishments. Those were bumpy rides in a rickety 1940s car. Amazed, she had gawked at mud huts festooned with crimson *ristras* and outside baking ovens called *hornos*, from which emerged loaves of fresh-baked bread. Brown-skinned women wearing mid-length dresses, their shoulders draped in blanket shawls, sat on the ground creating or displaying exotic-looking pots, earth-colored with white swirling designs etched in black. Linda wished they could have bought one of the beautiful pots; they sold for just pennies. Silver or beaded jewelry hung around the women's necks. Wide cloth belts cinched their dresses at the waist. Some wore high leather boots up to the bottom of their mid-length skirts, but many wrapped their legs in swaths of white cotton bunting, looking like the pictures of Egyptian mummies she'd seen in the storybooks provided by her mother.

Originally, she had planned to visit the three neighborhoods she had lived in, but as they neared the exit that would take them into the town, she suddenly decided to find only one, the spot where the adobe house of so many years before had stood. Perhaps the lovely old cottonwoods would be there, the kind she played under when she was four. Surprising herself, she felt a tug, an indescribable yearning to go home again.

"Mommy, tell me more about the little girl who drowned in the ditch near your house," Christi said, exhibiting a child's demand for the graphic details of morbid events. That story had come out when Christi, like all children, had begged, "Tell me about when you were a little girl." Sometimes Linda regretted relating that particular vignette.

"Why do you want to know about that, Christi?" Gripping the wheel, Linda turned and looked briefly at her daughter, wondering if she was still having the kind of bad dreams that plagued her after the separation from Larry. For months after the move to the Southwest, Christi had been fascinated with death and dying things.

"Well, I just want to hear the story again. And can you show me the ditch?" Christi said, displaying a familiar pout.

"She went wading, couldn't swim, and the water washed her away," Linda said, hoping her answer would satisfy.

"But *where* did she go?" Christi's relentless questions were tenacious and unsettling. "Did she go to heaven like my bunny did?"

Linda flashed on images of that day when the young girl was pulled from the irrigation ditch. Linda's parents had rushed to the scene because they wanted to be on hand to lend support, especially to the grieving parents who had lost a child. It was a scene best forgotten. People gathered round, murmuring and clucking. Later, one of her parents, she'd forgotten which one, had said, "They did bad things to her and then threw her in the ditch." What bad things? No answers came forth. But, not surprisingly, nightmares did.

In the days following the recovery of the body, she wondered if what her neighborhood friend Benny Rodriguez had told her was true. He said it was the ghost of La Llorona that caused the child to drown, that the girl had misbehaved in some way, disobeying her parents' warning not to go near the ditch. The story of La Llorona, or the Wailing Woman, was as much a part of Benny's culture as simmered beans and corn tortillas. In one version of the folktale, La Llorona, a beautiful woman jilted by her fiancé, became furious, and drowned her children, only to regret her deed. She then was doomed to wander the earth forever searching in vain for them. In another version, La Llorona kidnapped children who refused to obey their parents, especially admonitions about going close to rivers and ditches.

Linda's parents need not have continued the warnings forbidding her to go near the *acequia* which flowed close to that early home. What she had seen with her own eyes was enough to strangle any desire to climb up the ditch bank.

The experience left its mark. She avoided anything that would require her to duck her head under water. Her playmates were excited about taking swimming lessons, but Linda did not share their enthusiasm. She was frightened. But her mother volunteered to drive a small group from the neighborhood, brushing aside Linda's protests. Relief came swiftly, however. After the first lesson, the town pool had to close because of the polio epidemic sweeping the country. She did not learn to swim until she was in a college physical education class and then only by shutting off the past and concentrating on the dive. She thought it a miracle that she didn't drown, that she could rise to the surface and stroke to the edge of the pool. The phobia did not disappear during her years in California. She had refused to go swimming in the ocean. Larry had taunted her for that, unsympathetic to her water avoidance.

The swim in the motel three years before had been different. Stepping out of her past, Linda had felt the first taste of freedom, the beginning of liberation.

※

"All right, I'll see if we can find the ditch, but you have to be careful," Linda said. Despite her vow to avoid being too restrictive, here she was, sounding like her mother.

By sense alone, she knew how far to drive from Main Street. Approaching the main street of the town, Linda slowed her speed. There were no familiar landmarks. Gliding by what had been the only shopping area, she saw a McDonald's drive-in where once a boardwalk supported by wooden beams fronted the street, along which stretched a combination dry goods and grocery store. That was where her mother during those war years had counted out ration stamps for bacon, beans and flour, where she purchased Simplicity patterns and bolts of cloth to make their clothes. A Walgreens now stood at the corner where the local drug store used to be. There was no soda fountain as in her childhood, where the attendant whirled up – once the war ended and sugar was no longer rationed – her first strawberry malt.

Turning west onto a familiar residential street and later onto a dirt road, she drove slowly, by feel alone, toward the edge of town. Although houses and low-rise apartment buildings now blocked much of the landscape, there was enough open space to let her feel that she had been here before. Ahead she could see the hump of dirt forming the bank of the *acequia* and the familiar salt cedars and Russian olives running parallel along it, just as they were so many years ago. Her heart beat faster, and she pulled over on a wide shoulder of the road, cutting the engine and taking a deep breath. Christi bolted from the car, excited to be free, to join the sunshine and dig in the earth.

"I'm going to walk a little while, Christi. See what you can discover," Linda said. "Be careful, but be curious." Linda hoped to strike a balance between complete restriction for safety's sake and encouragement to explore new things. Christi quickly shed her shoes and raced away, leaving Linda alone in a billowing cloud of dust and a swarm of memories.

She was four again, awakening one day in May to the sun pouring its warmth all over her. To grow up in the Southwest is to know the sun well. Like a close friend who brings gifts, the sun had delivered reddish glints to her brown braids and painted freckles generously over her face and arms.

Their small adobe house was just a temporary rental, her mother said, until her father could get established in his business. Her mother was not comfortable with the Spanish-speaking neighbors and their strange foods. "Certainly not a proper diet," she said disparagingly, "for growing children." Reluctantly and uneasily, she let Linda play with the neighborhood children.

That morning Linda dressed hurriedly in blue cotton overalls and a short-sleeved blouse and slipped her feet into the brand new leather oxfords her mother had purchased in the city to the north. She wiggled her toes into the still-stiff leather, wishing that they didn't pull so tight around her ankles. She was ready to run outside and play, to swing, to imagine giants growing in the clouds and soldiers marching in the fields across the road.

She gulped oatmeal and crisp bacon and descended as fast as she could out of the chair stacked with books for a booster seat. As she headed toward door, her mother delivered the familiar admonition, "Don't ruin your brand new shoes. And don't ever, ever go near that ditch!"

As she bounded outside, grabbing her canvas hat and plastering it on her head, she saw her friend Benny Rodriguez, who was five, coming toward her from the next house over. He arrived, all smiles, bearing a peace offering, a ristra, for her mother, who smiled and thanked him for the string of crimson chili peppers. The two children galloped outside. At first, they took turns on the swing that her father had suspended from a tree in front of the house. Linda pumped high, her freckled nose wiggling, her blue eyes squinting at the sunbeams piercing the leaves. Back and forth, below her and in the distance, she saw the ditch streaming with dark brown water. Higher, higher – she could almost touch the purple hills! Copper braids flew until she slowed herself down. Then came a bump on the toe of her shoe as it skidded across the indent in the dirt, scuffing the leather and breaking her momentum.

She heeded her parents' warning about the ditch, but Benny ventured forth, descending to the forbidden canal and scooping up water in a tin can. Returning, he said, "See? No problem!" They fashioned forts and Indian pueblos with sticks and mud and peeled the green skin off the globes of fruit produced by the cottonwoods rimming the nearby ditch. Those pods were not quite ready to burst, but later in June, their silky strands would swell, break their shells and float around like cotton candy.

Her mother called them in when the sun was directly overhead and fed them a roast beef sandwich along with a glass of milk. When they ran outside, they found the clear blue sky of their morning now filling with clouds of all shapes. She and Benny studied them endlessly, fighting over whether they were trolls, dinosaurs or dragons. As the sun's rays softened in the afternoon, they slipped off their shoes and traced circles with their fingers in the dust. Pouring the can of water into the dirt, they dug their feet into the mud, squeezing the cool, grainy, rust-colored ooze through their toes.

Toward the end of the afternoon, she saw an old woman ambling by on the road, a black shawl wrapped around her shoulders. Innately curious, Linda ran out to the edge of the road to hear what was being said, but then realized that the woman was mumbling something in Spanish. Pointing beyond Linda's shoulder, the woman shook her head and shuffled off. When Linda turned around, she saw that Benny had disappeared. She had not been afraid, puzzled by her strange language, the one that Benny sometimes spoke with his family but not with her. And, oh, she needed to go back to the swing and put on her shoes before going into the house.

The shoes had disappeared. Frowning, she trudged back to the house barefoot, not knowing what she might be facing. The evening, filled with recriminations, ended heavily. Her mother thought the old woman had taken them. Her father offered the thought that Benny had snatched them away to play a prank. But the shoes never turned up, nor were they replaced that year. She recalled that for a long time she had to wear her canvas ones, the ones with the torn holes around the toes. There were no trips for a long time to the city to the north, for the shoes had been purchased with precious coins squirreled away by her mother. A new pair would have to wait.

Christi's shoes – where were they? In clouds of dust, she stooped to clutch a cake of clay. It broke, and tawny earth sifted through her fingers. Linda moved forward, feeling as though her feet were not touching the ground. In a daze, she climbed up the ditch bank. When she reached the top of the embankment, she looked down, eyeing cautiously the swift-racing waters. The hot sun told her this was no place to linger, so she side-stepped down the bank, seeking the shade of a nearby cottonwood tree

She had almost forgotten the special feel of this arid place: how utterly sun-drenched the earth, how thirsty the soil, how achingly blue the sky. A slight breeze ruffled the heart-shaped leaves of the cottonwood tree calling forth a whispering "whoosh, whoosh."

She stood transfixed staring at the tree, swaying with green globes waiting to burst their shells, to brush the air and brighten the ground. These were the fruits, she knew, of the female cottonwood. In days gone by she had thought of those silky strands as a nuisance but now was enchanted by their beauty. What she had overlooked before, she now saw clearly, for underneath their thick skins lay the potential for herself. She, too, could break open the shell that still lay submerged in her soul and cleanse it of any remaining despair.

Her mind whirled, and she felt her body both planted on the earth and dissolving somewhere she could not identify. Time boundaries disappeared and a sense of wholeness engulfed her. Here was a face-to-face encounter with the paradox of loss and loveliness. Here were memories of childhood pleasures and painful punishments. Here was the dreaded yet mysterious ditch, the flowing water of life and death. And here also were the cottonwood trees, with their promises of change and transformation.

※

"Mommy, I can see the ditch from here. Is that the one she drowned in?" Linda could hear Christi's voice but had lost sight of her.

"Up here! I'm up in the tree!" She had climbed onto one of the tree's lower branches, hoping to get a wider view of her surroundings.

"Just wait, Christi," she called and stumbled forward, catching in a blur a vision of her daughter's bobbing curls. By this time, Christi had eased herself onto a branch where Linda could reach her.

Her eyes blurred, then focused again. She reached up and pulled off a thin branch covered with the still developing hard pods.

"Are you crying, Mommy?" Christi asked as Linda lifted her down from the tree.

"It's all right," Linda said. "See if you can catch this." She tossed the twig to Christi, who scrambled for it. It pleased Linda that Christi was experiencing some of the same love of the earth, trees and sun which had befriended her when she was four. She felt the poignancy of childhood vanished, but saw in front of her the miracle of it recaptured and renewed. Pain and joy were all one, not separate. She could embrace both and take them inside to be part of her, forgetting bitterness, forgiving past wrongs.

She was already on her way, having left behind a destructive time in her life, creating a new path for herself, tracing the ruts and smoothing out the tread on her journey. As she saw Christi reliving some of her own childhood pleasures, she realized that priceless moments could happen again and again, one generation after another. She had come home again.

Home. Many times two impulses had warred inside of her – one, an intense desire to keep revisiting the past; the other, a wish never to think about what had vanished. The ambivalence was not rational but something compelling, deeper than intuition. Each time she tried to escape the memories, something tugged in her to return inexplicably to once-lived places, literally or in reverie. This "something" was deep, alternately begging at times to be submerged; at others, beckoning to be recreated.

Home was not just the physical spaces where she had grown up. Home was not something static. Home happened. Home happened whenever and wherever new growth took place. Home happened on the walk in the desert. Home happened at the dunes at the edge of the Pacific Ocean. Home happened in a swimming pool on a warm Arizona afternoon. Home happened in these very moments when she walked along the banks of an irrigation canal carrying water to thirsty crops.

Long ago, she had asked her parents about the little girl who drowned in the ditch, "Where did she go?" She had queried her father, "Did Grandmother go to heaven?" Christi wanted to know whether her bunny went to heaven. Where, or what, was heaven, after all? With time boundaries disintegrating, she knew the answer: Heaven was memory. Heaven was insight. Heaven was beauty and terror, sadness and joy. Heaven was both then and now. Heaven was home.

Growth and change; old roots, new forms. Linda and Christi, smiling broadly at each other, headed to the car.

Chapter Twelve
"You Are Not My Father"

Christi slipped out from under her sky blue comforter and squinted. Slicing through the blinds on her window, the sun threw stripes of light and shadow on the wall opposite her bed. The sun was so much more intense here. At first, she hated having to live in this dry, dust-filled climate. It had been over four years since the journey across the desert. Here there were no ocean waves splashing against the shore, no early morning fog dampening her T-shirts, no smell of eucalyptus trees swaying gently in the sea breeze.

Things were different, all right, but ever so slowly she was getting used to it and even looking forward to this new day. She glanced at the calendar on the wall. May 15, 1981. Into a new decade, a new era. Electronic music done on synthesizers had captured her interest along with punk rock. She was crazy about Pink Floyd, who was just coming on the scene. She had a new Mork from Ork Eggship transistor radio, a popular item since *Mork and Mindy* on TV was all the rage. She'd heard that exciting ways to reach the latest star performers were coming, without listening to the radio or watching television – devices with headphones so that you could pick and choose your favorite music.

She could not wait to get on her bicycle, the one she'd been given a few days ago for her eleventh birthday. The weather was perfect for bike riding. Cool morning temperatures, with a faint breeze rustling the leaves in the sycamores and elms dotting her neighborhood. Too nice to be in a windowless classroom taking spelling tests.

The bicycle had given her a new freedom. Instead of having to endure the ride on the school bus with kids who teased her, she now rode the bike to school, which was about two miles away. Only today, she didn't.

"Here's your breakfast. I fixed eggs and bacon for you," her mother called to her from the kitchen. "Come join us." *Us*, Christi knew, meant Matthew, her mother's new husband and Christi's stepfather.

She had never liked breakfast but to keep her mother from nagging, she took a few bites, then wiggled out of the chair, grabbing her glass of orange juice.

"Can't you ever be still?" Linda inquired, half-smiling, trying to assume a light-hearted tone. Her effort at gentle teasing fell flat. Christi frowned, then dashed out the door, ignoring the splashes of citrus liquid that fell on the green shag carpet.

Linda straightened up the house and was preparing to leave for the library when the phone rang. She glanced at the clock – 10:30. She needed to start work on her research project for the class she was taking at the university. She picked up the phone; it was the secretary at the elementary school. Christi had not arrived.

They had rehearsed the route along a main thoroughfare until some level of comfort about its safety was attained. Linda's frantic thoughts ran wild – abduction, accident, worse…What time had Christi left? About 8, in time to get to school for starting classes at 8:30.

Linda immediately called the police. "Missing eleven-year-old girl," she reported. "Wearing jeans and a blue T-shirt, blonde, petite, red bicycle, basket holding a backpack. Linda amazed herself at how calmly she reported the essential information.

"We'll get back to you," was the reply.

Any thoughts Linda had of working on her homework for class had to be abandoned. She dashed to her car and drove the route to the school, stopping occasionally. She got out and walked, checking behind trees, hoping not to find a scattered backpack or clothing. Nothing. Linda felt relief and panic intertwined.

Matthew also was concerned. He was home from the school where he taught because he was fighting off a cold. With Matthew, colds often went into bronchitis, so Linda had urged him to stay home.

Just after lunch, while Linda was washing up the dishes, the door opened. In walked a beaming Christi.

"Oh!" Linda's and Matthew's voices sounded in unison. Hugs and tears followed.

Christi announced triumphantly, "I rode all the way up the mountains. It was great!" She appeared to be oblivious to her transgression and exuded an air of confidence as if she had gained an educational lesson for the day, figuring it was a worthy proxy for her lapse in judgment.

"I even stopped at the big shopping center," she beamed. Why didn't her parents get the picture? They were just too much beyond her generation, she guessed, to understand the thrill of pedaling fast, feeling the air rush past her, ruffling her blonde curls.

Linda was too traumatized to know what to say or do. Hugging Christi close was all she could manage. Then she faced her daughter and said breathlessly, "Don't you know that it's against the law to skip school? What if the truant officer had caught you?"

Immediately regretting her words, she pressed Christi even closer to her. But Christi was pulling herself away, facing the two of them.

Matthew sneezed. "Damned cold," he muttered, retrieving a handkerchief from his pants pocket. But he stepped into the fray, knowing that Linda was distraught and dealing with overflowing relief. He was the logical one, especially in moments of crisis. He glanced at Christi, his face displaying concern but avoiding anything resembling reproach.

He calmly picked up the phone, called the police and canceled the alert. He turned to Christi, who stood in the middle of their wood paneled family room. Sunlight streamed in through the floor-to-ceiling windows, bouncing off bookcases, creating distorted shadows on all three faces, intensifying and magnifying each visage. They were faces that displayed – according to each person's response to the whole matter – shock, puzzlement or triumph.

Christi's four-foot, nine inch body was glued to the floor, legs firmly planted, hands on hips, blue eyes flitting between the two of them, silently inquiring, "Ok, now what? Punish me?"

Thinking he could appeal to an eleven-year-old's reasoning capacity, Matthew carefully chose his words and tone of voice. He avoided confronting Christi or pointing fingers at her, choosing instead to ignore her cocked head and lips curled downward into an enormous pout.

He reached out to touch Christi gently on the shoulder, but she jerked back, flattening herself against a wall of bookshelves. The force with which she had flung her backside sent books tumbling onto the carpet. Matthew bent down to pick up a copy of *Zen and the Art of Motorcycle Maintenance*.

Careful not to sound accusatory, he said calmly, "Do you know how frightened your mother and I have been?" He hoped to appeal to her empathy.

"Why? You're not my father!" Christi screamed. Dudley raced up to Christi, barking and brandishing his tail like a wagging finger.

Matthew motioned to Linda to pause, to just let silence reign for a while. Time to de-escalate.

Linda moaned inwardly at Christi's avoidance and denial. She felt frustration about her daughter's disregard for the concern for her welfare. She and Matthew shared that. It seemed to her that Christi saw these actions as entirely justified and thought of her parents as clueless. She also pondered the possibility that Christi magically believed that her report of the exhilarating adventure would absolve her transgression. But maybe Christi viewed the whole episode differently. She might have been terrified but expressed it by lashing out. Linda was not sure. Which was it?

The three stared at each other in silence. As Christi moved her eyes over their faces, Linda's mind raced, conjuring up reasons for Christi's temporary disappearance. Perhaps the bike ride was a purposeful act of defiance. Maybe it was payback for taking Christi away from everything she ever knew. Or, possibly it was simply another expression of Christi's inborn impulsiveness, the desire to experience some momentary excitement. She had always known Christi to be a child who reached out to grasp the world by the throat and make it work for her.

Christi fastened her glance on Matthew. "Aren't you listening? I told you, 'You are not my father'!"

Her voice shattered the silence, the pause in time when Linda's thoughts had taken her back to the life that she had left behind. Matthew, maintaining his calm, deflected Christi's answer.

"Your mother and I will be confiscating your bicycle for an indefinite period of time. And you will be riding the bus for a while." Christi cringed. Now *that* was a punishment.

"What's 'confiscating' mean? You always use big words!" she lashed out. "If you're going to take my bike away, just say so!"

Linda's and Matthew's eyes met again. Though no words were spoken, they seemed to communicate to each other their common understanding that Christi was acting as if she, and not her mother and Matthew, had been verbally attacked.

"You mean, you don't trust me," pouted Christi. It was as much a dare as a statement.

"Did your actions this morning lead us to trust you?" Matthew said. Christi scowled and stomped off to her room. Dudley padded after her.

Linda shot a pained look at Matthew. Feeling defeated, she commented, "I wonder what she'll cook up next."

Once in her room with the door shut, Christi plopped on her bed, fluffed up a pillow, and tried to cool down from the confrontation with her mother and Matthew. Dudley hopped up, and she stroked his smooth brown head, gently moving his ears back with her thumbs.

"He's not my father, he's not my father," she said aloud, as if it were a mantra. "And I *will* get my bicycle back." As she released Dudley, he appeared to nod at her.

※

As the years went by, more than once Christi recalled the day when she, carrying Dudley, climbed into the car, and her grandfather backed out of their driveway. The rain fell softly, like tears. The image of her father standing at the front door holding an umbrella grew smaller and smaller as the station wagon, stuffed with suitcases, lumbered down the hill.

At first she had been bewildered, with emotions ranging from anger to abandonment to apathy. There was even a bit of curiosity about the coming adventure. It had not occurred to her at the time to ask why Larry did not protest when her mother decided to move back to her hometown in the Desert Southwest. She wondered now if she had been dense, or just in shock.

For the first year, she and her mother lived in a small condominium complex, where she immediately met some girls her age. The friends of southern California gradually faded in her memory as she began to establish new relationships. She joined a soccer team and made even more friendships. She and her mother went to movies together, explored the city and ate out in restaurants serving real

New Mexican food, which was considerably different from the Tex-Mex dishes she had ordered in California. Chiles rellenos, chimichangas, carne adovada, guacamole, all tastier here, more *piquante*. She learned quickly that the waitresses would always ask, "Red or green"?

"Christmas," she learned to respond, meaning some of each type of chile. Then everything was polished off with fluffy sopapillas, fried puffy pastry, delicious with drizzled honey.

✥

The holiday season in New Mexico introduced even more new tastes and experiences but also resurrected sad memories because it was the day after Christmas that her mother and father had delivered the unbelievable announcement that they planned to divorce.

The year before that big earthquake in her life was the winter when she was six. She had begged her parents to take her into the nearby mountains to cut their own Christmas tree. It promised to be a splendid day for the three of them, crisp and cold with a sprinkling of snow as they climbed from sea level into the foothills east of the coast.

The area swarmed with people doing the same thing. Everyone was in jovial, festive spirits. Larry secured the proper permit, and together they roamed amongst evergreen trees with needles glistening on snow-covered branches. Christi thought it looked like an enchanted forest. Pine scent filled the air, mixing with a strong vanilla aroma from the ponderosas. Her parents wanted a moderate sized tree, one that they could lift without straining themselves, one that could be tied securely to the top of the car, but Christi begged for a giant one. Larry expressed some misgivings, but wanted to please her. He managed to wield the ax deftly and brought down an eight-footer.

"This one may scrape the ceiling," he said. "But, ok, we'll try it."

The three of them dragged it to the car, but they almost failed to hoist it on top and tie it down. Larry wrenched his back. Linda scraped her knee trying to be of help, but she rationalized that could have happened with a smaller tree, also. They ended the day drinking hot apple cider purchased at one of the stands catering to the tree-cutters.

After returning to their home near the Pacific Ocean and setting up the tree, they hung baubles and strings of lights. Her mother watered it faithfully every day and vacuumed up the pine needles that dropped to the carpet. Sometimes, before Linda could whisk them up, they stuck Christi's feet when she padded out to the living room in the morning. Outside, on the hills to the east, the lemon trees were bearing fruit.

Two days later, Christi fell ill with a case of strep throat. Her father was limping from the back strain caused by acceding to her wishes. Her mother played nursemaid to the two of them. On Christmas morning, the cookies and milk set out the night before were gone. She didn't even know why her mother had done that – Christi no longer believed in Santa Claus. Unenthusiastically, she emptied her stocking. Where had the magic gone?

❧❦

Having been transplanted to New Mexico, she had determined not to like anything about her new life, but despite those efforts, found herself falling in love with Christmastime in the Southwest, for it was celebrated in ways she had never known. Yes, she had seen luminarias in California, but not whole neighborhoods glowing from votive candles sitting on a pile of dirt inside a common paper sack. Her friends explained that this was a custom originating hundreds of years ago in the Spanish villages up and down the Rio Grande to show the way for the Christ child to appear in the world. But the best part about living here was getting together with friends and filling the sacks with dirt, arranging them along the sidewalks paralleling the street and up the walkways to front doors. As soon as the sun set, they could light the candles. One year a strong wind came up blowing over some sacks, which then caught fire. The candles burned down to the dirt quickly, eliminating the risk of flying sparks. Nothing could halt this yearly tradition, for luminarias would always defy the elements.

"You're so helpful, Christi," her mother told her, smiling. Christi lapped up the praise, feeling a joy she had not experienced for years, as the two of them joined in decorating the tree, and in baking several kinds of holiday cookies.

Her mother made huge pots of posole, a type of soup made with pork and hominy. On Christmas Eve, red-cheeked neighbors dropped in, flashing ready smiles and bringing cookies to share. A steaming kettle of mulled wine floating with orange peels, whole cloves and cinnamon sticks, sent spicy aromas throughout the house. Plates of cheese, guacamole and stuffed mushrooms lined the kitchen countertop. Conviviality and good wishes reigned. On these occasions, Christi felt wrapped in a warm blanket of something indefinable, something rare and comforting, an emotion she realized had eluded her in what she once had believed to be her perfect childhood.

When she was going on nine, just when she and her mother were getting along better, putting some of the pain of the past behind them, another person emerged in their lives, a man named Matthew whom her mother had known from years back. Matthew sometimes came over in the evening and they would all play scrabble or card games together. Matthew started showing up with her mother at her soccer games, with both of them cheering her on. Then, in time, to no one's surprise, including Christi, he married her mother, and they became a family.

She liked Matthew. He told funny stories and always included her in the conversation. He asked what she thought about things, the state of the world, what was going on in her life. Matthew taught her how to make the sugar water for the hummingbird feeders. They loved watching the rufous hummingbirds buzz around, chasing the small ones away, and often laughed together as this more aggressive species zoomed in, determined to be the only ones to roost on the feeders.

Matthew introduced her to *Nova* on television, and he found pictures in *National Geographic* that he thought she'd particularly like, such as sharks and dolphins. She got to accompany her mother and Matthew to the movies. A special favorite, which she watched wide-eyed, was *Star Wars*.

Matthew and her mother bought a three-bedroom home in the same general area, situated on enough land so that Matthew could have a garden and Dudley would have a large fenced yard. Christi could maintain the friendships she had already developed and attend the same school in which she was enrolled.

Her life took on predictability. She fed Dudley, took him for walks, and began to assume more responsibility for household chores. She sometimes helped Matthew weed and plant in the garden. That first summer in the new house yielded peppers and green beans, cantaloupes and strawberries. Together, she and Matthew harvested the wild asparagus that grew naturally, and her mother taught her how to steam it.

She began learning to play the flute in her junior high school band and taking piano lessons from a gentle older man who patiently tried, without success, to teach her to read notes. She was too impatient, having a natural gift. Once she astonished her mother by playing the familiar part of *Für Elise* by ear from hearing it on the classical music radio station.

Christi noticed that her mother's attitude had mellowed, that she was not as persistently judgmental and critical as she had been in California. On occasion, though, eruptions occurred if there was a failure to straighten up a messy bedroom or remove a left-behind pair of shoes from the hallway. Her mother was just too strict about neatness, she thought, grumbling to herself.

Though renewed happiness filled her life, trouble came along with the joy. She resented Matthew when he backed up her mother in denying what the two of them believed to be an unreasonable request. No longer could she play her parents off against each other. Sometimes, clinging to old habits, she tried, causing difficulties for herself and her newly formed family. To be sure, she sometimes failed to do her chores, but, she thought, it wasn't that she was spiteful, just distracted. She was dismayed when Matthew, even gently, suggested that she needed to be more responsible.

"But I do," she protested. Sometimes she felt as if she could do nothing right, that it was impossible to live up to her mother's standards. She believed that her mother was just too stuffy and strict, and Matthew, while nice, was often too cautious and boring. Her dad was the hip one, the one she wanted to emulate.

Although sour moods did not dominate her life, they came often enough. She constantly tested the boundaries, and when she was denied something she wanted to buy or to do that Matthew and her mother felt was not appropriate, she resorted to the same words used on the day she rode away on her bike. She slung them at Matthew, intending to wound.

"I don't have to obey you! You're not my father! My father is in California and I want to go back and live with him!"

Chapter Thirteen
One Cool Dad

Before they decided to marry, Linda had warned Matthew, "Christi came to believe that she was a golden princess deserving of anything she wanted. Larry always gave in to her, but I'm partly responsible, too. Whenever I'd try to the draw the line, Larry did not back me up, and I caved rather fight him on it. I just wanted you to know, because she has a real adjustment coming."

She told Matthew that Christi had learned from an early age how to wheedle and win. Toys, trips, designer jeans – she could talk her father into any of it. His only requirement was for her to say that she would be "good." Then Larry would disappear into his work downtown and his tennis games on the weekend leaving her, Linda, to deal with an increasingly demanding Christi. Good? What did that mean? Linda explained to Matthew that she made a stab at trying to spell it out with lectures on manners, on asking rather than demanding, even though she knew that was not the way to get through to a young child.

"I found myself treating Christi the way my mother had treated me. And I hated it," she added. "I tried time out for bad behavior. That didn't work. Then I would deny her an afternoon with friends. That was not successful, either. Christi had a mind of her own from Day One. And I was conflicted. I didn't want her to be disliked by people because of her behavior, but, you know, I did admire her determined spirit. She spoke her mind, something I wish I had done when I was growing up."

Linda paused, and then continued. "In many ways she's a really great child. She knows what she wants out of life, and she'll tell you. She was a happy child but began to change as Larry and I became more distant, and when he was no longer there for her. I think, also, that I was pretty rough on her during that time. I really regret that."

Matthew nodded, as if he understood Linda's remorse that things had not gone better for her and Christi. Matthew was older than Linda and, having raised four children, allowed for a wide range of behavior according to their disparate personalities. But he drew the line when it came to safety. He did not tolerate lame excuses and maintained that it was important that kids live up to their responsibilities.

"She definitely is challenging, but I do care for her, and I hope that she will see that some day," he said, seeking to reassure Linda that Christi's "moments" were a phase, due to pass in time.

Matthew was eager to take Christi on camping trips. His own children had loved to camp and fish, and he had mistakenly assumed that his new stepdaughter also would enjoy the outdoors. But Christi was not destined to become a convert.

On a trip to the Grand Canyon, Christi and her friend Kathy complained about the inconveniences of tent camping, especially the bathroom facilities. They spent most of their time with hair brushes and compacts, applying makeup on their pre-teen faces.

"I don't get this," Matthew said, shaking his head in frustration. "This wonder of the world, its immensity, its incredible depth and subtle colors. All lost on them. Maybe we should just turn around and go home."

Ignoring Matthew's disappointment, Christi turned to him and announced, "Well, not everyone is into nature. I just happen to like other things." Clearly, on this point, she and Matthew would never see eye to eye.

Linda, too, was exasperated after all the effort to prepare for the camping trip. She could only hope that in time, as Matthew had suggested, Christi might come to have a wider view of the world. But she knew the trail to that might be long and winding.

Desert Daughter

Larry as usual picked her up at the airport. This particular visit took place between her junior and senior years of high school. She had just turned seventeen. She was looking forward to beach time, tennis playing, visiting, just being with her father and having him introduce her to all his affluent and cool friends. Larry had been reinventing his life back in California. He had remarried, joined a prestigious beach club, and shied not at all from flaunting his worldly success. She enjoyed these visits with her father and his wife Betty. Larry always took vacation time when she came for the week, but things had been different in the last two years. He showed less and less interest in her and her life, but she figured that was to be expected since he saw her only one time per year.

Betty never failed to be cordial. Her daughters Susan and Jean always welcomed Christi into their circle of friends and activities, but Christi never felt that she fit in. She envied their lifestyle of ease and comfort, playing tennis all day, swimming in the ocean, doing barbecues on the beach. This was the life for her, not the mundane days of soccer and school work and playing with her unsophisticated friends back in New Mexico. No, she aspired to be a suave charmer molded into that role by her upwardly mobile father.

She once had envisioned her father clamoring to regain custody of her. That did not happen, and though she wondered why he invited her out only once per year, she did not sway in her belief that one day he would move to claim her.

Now, newly arrived for her yearly visit, she unpacked her suitcase and changed into a black T-shirt and jeans because she knew that her father loved black. She entered the living room to find her father, as usual, with a drink in his hand.

He beckoned for her to come nearer, stretching out his hand. Surprised, she saw that there were several bills. "Here's some money." He handed her some $20 bills. "Who's that friend you meet up with here? Ask her out and go bar hopping." He had winked at her and laughed.

"Cool," she said, flashing a wide smile, "What a cool dad." She hugged him.

The summer before, she had revealed to him that she had acquired a fake ID. Those early paper driver's licenses were easy to doctor up. Just slit the picture carefully and insert your own. Half the time, the ID checkers in those places barely glanced at you, just the birthday listed on the card.

At first, she had been reluctant to admit to her father that she'd bought the license from Diana, the older sister of her friend Leslie back home. Christi knew that Diana needed cash to buy weed. Christi had tried it along with the two sisters. Everyone in her group had passed around a joint, but that vice did not have its pull for her. On the other hand, alcohol did. And everyone was getting fake IDs and going out to bars. So, of course, that made it even more exciting – to be daring and not get caught. Never once did she figure that would happen to her. Never once did she have qualms about flouting the law.

Instead of reprimanding her, Larry seemed impressed by her boldness. Although he had always prided himself on having the highest ethics and moral standards, something had slipped along the way. At one time, his motto was *do the right thing*. It had been replaced with *dare to defy*.

Later, when she was older, she would wonder what he had been thinking. He had never before been the type to advocate breaking the law. Such a straight arrow, her mother had always said, one of his good points. Yet he had suggested that she go off on her own, knowing that she was shy of the legal age. She recoiled thinking about how both of them could have been fined, hauled into court, or worse. It appalled her to think that she did not question his actions or her own.

That was the same summer that Larry had given her money to buy a black bathing suit. Looking her up and down as she modeled it, he told her bluntly, "You're too fat. Too many chimichangas in that backwater place where you live?"

She felt denigrated, uncertain why her perfect father, the one that used to play with her in the ocean waves, was teasing her, humiliating her so much that she stood there tongue-tied, unsure of how to respond. She knew she was a bit overweight, but she had not considered herself gross. Then reality smacked her in the face. She was becoming an embarrassment to him.

His words had stung more than she could bear. Maybe he had forgotten that when she performed in her ballet recital at age six, pert in a pale blue tutu and ballet slippers, she was the heaviest of all the girls, not egregiously so, but noticeably. It came as a shock to think that her father saw her as ugly. Well, she had eyes, too. Her father himself was getting a bit paunchy. His blond hair was thinning, but he still retained his marvelous tan, which he worked at assiduously by going to the beach as often as possible, rubbing himself all over with coconut oil.

He wanted her to be something she was not, even though she, unlike her mother some years before, would have been happy to transform herself into his ideal image. Her natural hair color was medium blonde, but he encouraged her to use more peroxide. A California girl has to look the part, he said. She returned to New Mexico after one of those visits, stepping off the plane, shocking her mother and Matthew, smiling at them with a face encircled in a shining halo of platinum hair glinting like shafts of sunlight off ice.

Comprehension of the subtext of her father's messages penetrated more slowly than it should have. He really did not want her around. The cash. The encouragement to go bar hopping. Buying her off, just to get her out of the house. He had no idea how to relate to her. He never asked her what she did in school or what she did in her free time. Nor did she volunteer any but the most superficial details about her life in New Mexico. She knew that he would find it uninteresting compared to the glamorous life he and Betty were leading.

She reminded herself of those days growing up in glitzy southern California. How she managed to get him to buy everything she wanted, from designer clothes and shoes to trips to Disneyland to the latest tech toys. How she scoffed at her mother who tried to substitute what she considered important things like trips to the local library, art museums, musical concerts, walks in the many parks in their city. These were all right, sometimes even fun. But unquenchable materialism overwhelmed it all, and her father's values won the day.

In a burst of understanding, Christi became convinced that her father was an alcoholic. On the visit last year, just before she entered college, he had driven her around Orange County in his new BMW, bragging about the built-in bar, a renovated glove compartment. He would reach down and open it, grab a one-ounce bottle of vodka, and take a swig. Then he would step on the gas, sending the car into a swerve, just missing a vehicle whizzing by them on the freeway. At the time, Christi had not been the least bit concerned. It was so daring, so posh, so with it, she had thought. Now she shuddered to realize what might have happened. Amazing, she saw in retrospect, that he had not been pulled over by the police.

She began to see the truth of his life. A glimmer of enlightenment began to penetrate her consciousness, the possibility that her mother had seen the same thing and that was part of her reason for leaving the marriage. She tried to explain to her mother how he was, but omitted the part about the fake ID and the rides in the bar-equipped automobile. But she did reveal that he spiked his juice in the morning, then brushed his teeth with mint toothpaste to camouflage the tell-tale breath. She saw him down several scotch and waters before and after dinner. And Betty always served wine with the evening meal. In the interim, he worked at his office. No telling what he consumed there.

∾❦∽

More than ten years had passed since taking that trip across the desert. Christi was eighteen now, a freshman at a small women's college in the Midwest. In her dorm room while her roommate was away at classes, she crinkled the foil-lined wrapping encircling the square of Ex-Lax and popped it in her mouth. She had been doing this for several months. She stretched out on her bed, right on top of the red and white quilt. She loosened her jeans. Yes, they were getting too tight.

Last night she had stuffed herself with Chinese food – lo mein, tons of noodles with shrimp, chicken, beef – followed by a whole package of Oreo cookies when she got back to her dorm room. Sometimes it was Godiva chocolates. But this time, Oreos. She had gained more than the "freshman fifteen" her college friends laughed about. And she knew that she shouldn't gain any more. None of her clothes were fitting. Ex-Lax was her answer to rid herself of her indiscriminate and voracious eating habits. So was her finger, at times stuck down her throat after gorging on carbs. Short-term problem. Solved.

She had a history of eating food to excess, far after her hunger was satisfied. When she was five, at a family holiday dinner her mother had set out extensive hors d'oeuvres since the turkey was taking longer than normal. There were cheese balls, stuffed mushrooms, cream cheese with chili jam, and ham loaf and crackers. Christi's cousins retreated to her bedroom to play games, but Christi instead circled around the card table, grabbing something of each specimen, stuffing it into her mouth. She did not stop eating, and when the Thanksgiving dinner was served at last, she loaded her plate with turkey, stuffing, mashed potatoes and gravy. Later that day, as her mother was bidding good-bye to her guests, Christi turned pale and tugged at her mother's skirt. Knowing exactly what was about to happen, Linda scooped up Christi and ran with her to the sink. Up came everything, the excesses of the entire afternoon.

Activities in high school brought a reprieve, for she had been active in soccer, swimming and cheerleading. She kept her weight at an appropriate level without effort. Life was good. But the dark side began to emerge. Just when all was going well, she began drinking with her friends, and several times she misjudged and consumed too much. Once she even had to go to the hospital emergency room to have her stomach pumped. But she continued to drink even more in college, especially at the far-too-frequent fraternity parties.

Sitting on her bed, exhausted after spending time in the bathroom, she found her mind whirling memories like a tumble dryer full of sheets, panties and bras, T-shirts and jeans. Spinning around with the illusions of clothing rotating in a maddening repeating rhythm, was a wadded up ball of remorse and fright.

She was facing up to the fact that she had an eating disorder and that she was either now an alcoholic or heading in that direction. For a long time, she had denied bingeing and then purging, denied that she had passed out from drinking too much. Now she was seeing a counselor who was helping her try to uncover the reasons for her behavior. The next step, her therapist suggested, was to discuss her problem with her parents. Time to stop hiding.

Her mother and Matthew did not know the half of it, but they sensed that something was terribly wrong. When she did come home on breaks, she was quieter than usual, distant, distracted. She viewed her parents as so naïve, so trusting. Still, she knew they wanted the best for her, and she gave them credit for giving her respect as a late teen, nearly a young adult. But her withdrawn behavior was not lost on them. They had been reluctant to pry, for which she was grateful. She knew they would be terribly disappointed in her. She wanted to stop doing all this but could not find the key to breaking the cycle.

Food. Alcohol. Sex. Too much of everything, she knew. And she didn't even like them, any of them. What was wrong with her? She was in emotional turmoil. She did not know how she was going to explain what she had been doing with her life. She made decent grades in the college she attended, but how could she reveal the sordid stories of the drinking binges or her shame of waking up in an unfamiliar bed and knowing that one of the fraternity boys from the nearby university had had sex with her. The party at the fraternity house had been fun, alive with jokes and laughter, but after that, her memory blurred. Missing were the details of how she found herself naked under a sheet and saw that her clothes were flung about the room. So it must have been that. Had this happened multiple times? Appalled, she had no idea. Never the praying type, she now thanked God that she had not become pregnant.

She began to wonder: What is real and what is fake? What am I doing here? Am I living in a dream? What path am I on and where does it lead?

"Fuck!" she screamed and pounded her fist against the Red Hot Chili Peppers poster decorating her dorm room.

※

She tossed in bed until the covers twisted around her body. Beads of sweat sat like dewdrops on her forehead and upper lip. Her underarms were damp, with rivulets beginning to flow and stain her nightgown. She was dreaming of a banquet, with the allure of a bounty of food. But on the table appeared hideous insects, writhing in dishes. Even in her sleep, she groaned, feeling both attraction and revulsion. She woke up, ran to the bathroom and vomited.

Chapter Fourteen
The Place You Go

Christi dropped out of college, burdened with shame. Having completed one year and one semester, she came home during Christmas break and announced that she would not be returning.

She carried around the feeling that she was a loser, that she would never dig herself out of this pit. The words from her favorite song, *Comfortably Numb*, by Pink Floyd, spoke volumes about the way she felt about herself. Those final lines rolled around in her head: *When I was a child/ I caught a fleeting glimpse/Out of the corner of my eye/I turned to look but it was gone/I cannot put my finger on it now/The child is grown/ The dream is gone/I have become comfortably numb.*

Matthew and Linda hid their dismay and tried to be supportive, telling her that they had confidence she would figure out what she needed to do with her life. As they talked about how they might be of help to Christi, Linda recalled the poem by Robert Frost with its famous line about what home is – "the place where, when you have to go there, they have to take you in." But that wasn't the case here, Linda and Matthew agreed. They did it willingly, with hopes that Christi would be able to heal from whatever pain she was suffering.

While living temporarily with her mother and Matthew, Christi began to assess her life, slowly gaining strength to steer it in another direction. She joined a help group for her alcohol problem and returned to a university closer to home and graduated with a degree in her chosen field. Her career prospects looked bright.

One year after getting her college degree, her father's brother telephoned to report the news that her father had taken his own life in an alcohol rehabilitation center.

Christi did not grieve for long; with distance and time, she had begun to see her father for what he really was.

But something continued to nag at her, the way she had treated Matthew, the obsession she had with her father Larry, whom she now saw as shallow and unfeeling. Somehow, she wanted to make amends for the slinging of insults, the breaking of rules. How blind she had been to Matthew's patience with her!

She approached her mother alone one day with a startling idea. "I want to let Matthew know I think of him not as my stepfather but as my *real* father. Do you think he might adopt me?"

Stunned but enormously pleased, Linda passed along Christi's message to Matthew.

"Well," he gulped, "let's get together and talk about this."

"And would you believe, she wants to do it at our church, in front of our minister," Linda said, still astonished by the news.

She got in touch with Christi and invited her to come over and tell Matthew face-to-face about her feelings.

Looking straight at Christi, Matthew placed his hands on both her shoulders, and said simply, "Why not?" His brown eyes twinkled with pleasure.

Christi threw her arms around Matthew, looking at him tenderly as her blue eyes brimmed with tears.

"You know, Christi, you have made me very happy, and your mother, too." He removed his glasses and reached for a handkerchief in his pocket.

On the scheduled day, they arrived at the church and entered the sanctuary. The minister opened with kind words about the meaning of "family." Then, as planned, Linda began to read a letter she had prepared.

Desert Daughter

April, 1992
Dear Christi,

 This is your story. I admire your courage in taking hold of your life and charting a new direction for yourself. Your journey has not been easy. But, true wisdom comes not from skipping easily on a cleared pathway, but from untangling the brambles that catch and threaten to contain you.

 You arrive in our household the year after Neil Armstrong walks on the moon. Finally, after ten years of marriage, we are now a family of three. Your dad treats you as a cute new plaything. Until you are about four, he is, for being a "workaholic," an involved weekend family man. We take you with us almost everywhere, even on driving trips, and you charm everyone en route. Then it all stops. Something else begins to surface, his gradually increasing interest in alcohol. I overlook this and mistake the trend as normal. An ominous sign, it leads to a major change in our family.

 It is the day after your seventh Christmas. With dread, I break the news to you that your father and I will be getting a divorce. I hate doing this to your tender soul. I know I have shattered your sense of security, and I fear for what might lie ahead for both of us. In April we set out for New Mexico in my Toyota station wagon – you and I, your grandfather and Dudley, the dachshund. During many hours of traveling through the desert, I think about how I will raise you as a single mom. What have I done?

 We get settled in a small southwestern style apartment with brick floors, adobe walls and a beehive fireplace. On the patio, in a strip of flowerbeds, someone has planted hollyhocks. Huge cottonwoods shade our west window, a blessing I know will be welcome when the summertime heat arrives.

 Spring comes to the Southwest in stages. Crocuses and grape hyacinths appear first, then daffodils. Globe willows are the first of the trees to show new leaves, turning from tan to vivid yellow-green, and forsythia bushes suddenly burst out in a stunning array of yellow blooms. Apple blossoms splash over the dry, tan earth, and robins hop on newly sprouted and sprinkled lawns, pecking and searching for worms. The sky is bluer, the cumulus clouds whiter and puffier than you have known on the seacoast. You tell me you like this spring. We are making progress.

The second spring brings yet another miracle. His name is Matthew Benjamin Woodward. A long-time friendship from years back blossoms into romance. You like him, and you beg us, please, please get married. You want so much to be a family again. Matthew wants to help parent you also. He wants to take you camping, to show you the wonders and beauty of nature, to share visits to museums and monuments. He is a teacher both professionally and personally, a good man, a family man. He starts attending your soccer games and hears you play your flute in school performances. He introduces you to his children, and they enthusiastically incorporate you into their, now our, family.

This change in lifestyle and values is a shock to your system. You cooperate with the new family dynamics and responsibilities some of the time, but often you lash out. You tell Matthew that he is not your father and that he cannot tell you what to do. You fantasize that your father back in California will take you away, let you live with him. He tells you the blunt truth, that this will not happen. But you do not believe him. He rejects your plea to visit him more frequently, such as during school breaks for holidays or for longer visits in the summer. You are crushed but hold onto the belief that he will change his mind.

Matthew and I are blessed with sufficient material necessities of life. We feel fortunate to provide a comfortable though not luxurious home for you. But we do not value the same kinds of things that mean so much to your father.

Periodically, you rebel, turn sullen and become devious. We worry that we cannot reach you. We tell each other that you are a pre-teen and that you have experienced many losses. We think you are looking for the perfect father. We hold on, offering our unconditional love.

It takes many years and much reflection on your part to put the fantasy completely to rest. You belong to us. Sometimes you show that you know this and appreciate the fact, but other times, you pull away. As the years pass, you make some good choices and some unfortunate ones. Matthew exudes compassion. He, as well as I, will not let you go.

Shocking news reaches us just as you are beginning to resolve your many conflicted feelings. We learn that Larry, your father, has taken his own life after descending into severe alcoholism. You are adult enough to now to see how empty his life really was. Your exact words, delivered with little emotion, are, "I can't even feel sad. He was so pathetic."

Later, after absorbing this news, you ask if you can talk to me, alone. You arrive bearing a courageous question. "Do you think that Matthew would adopt me?" Matthew is moved by your gesture, and we discuss what we might do. He approaches you, "Would you like me to adopt you legally or symbolically?" You think about it and we discuss the pros and cons. Finally, we decide together that we will not go through legal steps, but that we will do a brief ceremony at our church because we think it will be a memorable one for all of us, like a baptism or a christening ceremony. It is recognition of the conscious choice to be born again into a new life.

So that is why we are here today, to put to rest all the fantasies you ever held about fatherhood, because you realize that what you sought was always there. You just had to let in the light. This ceremony confirms what has been true for you for a long time. It is your chosen way to recognize that the real dad is the one who stays the course through years of caring and support. You have asked your family and our

pastor to be with you as you publicly recognize this very special relationship. I can think of nothing more sacred.
With deepest love,
Mom

To conclude the service, at that point, Matthew, displaying a picture frame with text carefully done in precise calligraphy, stepped forward and read:

Given to Christi Marie Sanders on the occasion of her adoption as a daughter by Matthew Benjamin Woodward. In one of your favorite books, The Velveteen Rabbit, *the skin horse says that you become real when someone loves you, and once you become real, you don't ever become unreal again. You have proclaimed me your real father. I now hereby proclaim that you are my real daughter, just as your mother is your real mother. May the blessings of life and love come your way as you journey onward.*
—Matthew Benjamin Woodward
Proud father of Christi Marie Sanders

Christi, like her mother, but in her own way and by her own choice, had come home.

Chapter Fifteen
Letting Go

Only by acceptance of the past can you alter it.
     – T.S. Eliot

June, 1992

After her father's death, Linda returned to her life in Colorado. But one task remained, her mother's request to dispose of the ashes. That meant yet another trip to New Mexico.

"I don't have the energy to figure this out. Would you do it?" Her mother's voice was neither plaintive, nor sad, just matter-of-fact. Once her husband was gone, she simply had no interest in his remains.

But Linda had procrastinated, not certain of the motives for her hesitation. When nearly a year had elapsed, she knew from some deep part within her exactly what she wanted to do.

"I'd like to place some of his ashes in this box I've kept for so many years. You know, the one that your friend Isabel gave me when I was a child?" Linda said.

"Oh, I didn't know you kept that! Such a little thing, that gift of the box. I thought you would have gotten rid of it years ago," her mother said. "What do you remember about our friend Isabel?"

"That she was tall, elegant, and her gorgeous black hair was piled high on her head and fastened with the most interesting combs. One of them had glittering diamonds and pearls. I had never seen anything like that. I thought she was the most beautiful and exotic woman I had ever seen. You told me that at her marriage to Miguel she wore a mantilla. I always thought of her that way, as a bride wearing a mantilla."

"You probably remember that Miguel was the assistant district attorney and his marriage to the beautiful Isabel Mendoza was the talk of the town," her mother responded. "I saw their wedding announcement in the local paper. Isabel was from a prominent family in Santa Fe. I always wondered whether she would like living in that small town."

Linda recalled the evening that Isabel and Miguel came to join Linda's parents for a game of bridge. Her father had bustled around setting up the table and chairs, ignoring Linda's presence. Her mother was busy cutting up cheese for snacks.

"I'll put the plate of cheese and crackers on the table," she recalled telling her mother.

"You might drop it. So I'll do it," her mother said, brushing her aside.

Her mother expected perfection, and of course, Linda could never measure up, and her father also never hesitated to point out her clumsiness.

It occurred to Linda now that Isabel possibly had noticed how this somewhat-in-the-way child was left out, for Isabel had smiled and handed Linda the diminutive chest along with a key and whispered, "Take a look inside."

Decorated with metal swirls that looped over the hill of the curved lid, it was secured with a clasp. In the keyhole was a tiny key. Excitedly, Linda had opened the hasp and peered in. There a small swatch of lace from Isabel's mantilla and a black and white picture of her and Miguel, his arm draped around her. Both were tall. Both were beaming. Underneath the picture was a 1945 Mexican gold coin.

"For me?" Linda gasped.

"Yes, for you. May you find happiness, beauty, love. These are your treasures."

"And money?"

"Of course – but the real gold is not in the coin."

What had Isabel meant?

Her mother's voice interrupted the momentary memory flash. "Well," she huffed, "I knew she was glamorous. I did the best I could under the circumstances."

Then, shifting the conversation abruptly in a less prickly tone, she continued, "You knew, didn't you, that Miguel was your father's lawyer? We lost touch with them after your father's business went bankrupt and we moved."

Her mother sounded defensive, and Linda realized she might have crossed a delicate line by saying that Isabel was the most beautiful woman she had ever seen. The words had come out awkwardly, not intending to hurt but having that effect. Although there was unspoken love between them, specific words of affection were rarely uttered. They took each other very much for granted.

Linda had not wished to divulge that she had kept the treasure chest, for she thought her mother might ask why she had retained this relic all these years. She did not want to have to explain the notes and jottings, tucked away, in which she had poured out all her bitterness about her misunderstandings with her parents. In the chest, the piece of mantilla lace had yellowed over the years, and the picture had curled and cracked. She wished now that she had kept them but at some point had tossed them out along with the revealing notes. But the gold coin never lost its luster. She had removed it and put it in a black velvet pouch, hiding it safely in a drawer so that it could travel with her wherever she went.

Covering her face to prevent inhaling gray powder, Linda spooned a small portion of her father's bone dry ashes from the cardboard box into the diminutive casket. She did not tell her mother what she planned to do but rather tried to reassure her.

"I'll take care of the remainder as you asked," she said.

"We have a plot in the Heritage Gardens, here in town, for both of us. I suppose you can arrange for the burial there," her mother said.

It would be her last trip to the place where she and Christi had visited. So much of her childhood had begun right there, where her father's decisions had set her destiny in motion. It was only fitting to return for a final visit. A portion of her father needed to be there.

She motored south down the interstate, exiting about half an hour after leaving Albuquerque. First she drove to the train station where the ill-fated carloads of ore had rumbled off to their ill-gotten destination. Railroad cars and engines sat on the tracks, and in the distance she could hear the plaintive whistle of an approaching locomotive.

Not too far away, she located the street with the frame house – now gone – near the church and park. She recalled the day when the family had moved from the adobe house, taking up residence now as respectable townspeople. Perhaps her mother and father were excited, but all she could think of was taking a last look at the swing, its knotted ropes and smooth wooden seat dangling from the gnarled cottonwood tree. The second house was where her kitten had disappeared and where children had driven needles into her palms. Driving slowly down familiar streets, Linda spied the building that had been the community church of her childhood. She had run up and down those steps, causing her mother to be chastised for not controlling her daughter. The church was now a funeral home.

She left that neighborhood and headed west, to what used to be far outskirts of the community. She wanted to drive by the stately old Catholic church. It was there, looking from the outside just at it did so many years ago. Why, it's just a brown, ancient building with a steeple, she thought. But it held a special place in her memory. Here was the place where her neighborhood friends took their First Holy Communion. She had attended by invitation one of the ceremonies, dutifully covering her head with a scarf. Afterwards, she had begged her mother for a white taffeta dress and wondered why she could not be Catholic. She envied them. The priest touched their foreheads with holy water; and they carried candles, rosaries and little white Bibles. She was strongly attracted to the drama and mystery that happened inside those walls. In those days she was always reaching for something else, something vibrant beyond what she considered to be her ordinary life, missing in all its drabness some semblance of personality, spark and joy.

Back to Main Street for another search, the place where her father's photography studio had once been, but it was hard to discern the exact spot since that block had been rebuilt and several small businesses occupied the area – a beauty salon, print and copy shop, Chinese restaurant, a liquor store and a fitness center.

At the south edge of town, she turned west from Main Street on the now-paved road leading to her old neighborhood, to the house near the end of the road, the last home lived in before the move back to Albuquerque. She drove slowly, hoping that anyone seeing her would not mistake her for someone stalking the neighborhood. The house, inhabited by her family over forty years ago, was still standing, its porch askew, a torn screen door flapping in the breeze. The once-green trim was now turquoise but weathered and peeling.

Much of the front yard including the cherry tree had been taken for avenue expansion so that now the house sat close to the street. She could see from her car the still unfenced backyard, with two well-worn concrete steps. Long ago, so long that memory had both receded and recurred as if it were yesterday, she saw herself playing jacks and marbles on those steps, imitating movie stars, and reading her precious books, the stories that transported her into enchanted lands.

And then, on to the final stop. Linda continued driving slowly west toward the river until neighborhoods disappeared and the area became more rural with clumps of thick, familiar cottonwoods.

Parking the car on a dirt shoulder, she swung her legs out of the driver's seat and stretched her body toward the sun. Around the trees, wisps of clouds floated. Clouds? No, something else. The blue sky had turned into a feathery whiteness. She approached the tree and something tickled her nose and brushed her skin. She snapped off a twig drooping with fresh green capsules, their weight pulling down the branches. They were bulging, and many had already split, sending out seedlings and turning the blue sky into a whiteness of floating feathers, ephemeral as life. With the torn end, she drew a spiral in the dirt. Not a closed circle, but something open to suggest that life held surprises yet to come.

It was tranquil here, the sky shimmering with radiance, the air filled with the earthy scents of spring. Across the ditch she could see long rows of green alfalfa and hear in the distance the coo-woo-wooing of a mourning dove. Then, quiet. She listened, loving the silence. Then came the ethereal song of a meadowlark.

She peered up and over the low dirt bank of the *acequia*. By this time, some of these canals had been concrete lined, but not this one. It was the same as it had been in her childhood. She was grateful that urbanization here had encroached only slightly.

Carefully lifting the treasure chest out of the car, she set it under a cottonwood tree, where she stopped for a moment, recalling her swing and the brown-ribboned ditch, and the one nearly perfect day with Benny Rodriguez, until it ended with a scolding over the loss of her shoes.

During that time here with Christi twelve years ago, she had been overwhelmed by the feeling of oneness of everything. With time suspended, the entire collection of memories and emotions had blended into a rare experience of transcendence. Afterwards came the strong impulse to hold on to that elusive moment, if only fleetingly, for there was a flash of certain knowledge that it might not ever come again. But its power would be cocooned forever within her heart and mind until, like all things, she ceased to be a breathing, living being.

Reverie. Memory. Action.

Now, she retrieved the miniature casket and moved slowly toward the ditch, the twig grasped firmly in her hand, thinking about all the journeys she had taken in her life to this point. Each step had brought yet one more grain of wisdom. From her early married life, there had been the two trips to the dunes, one brimming with anticipation, the other simmering with conflict. There had been indecision and doubts, never knowing what the pounding waves might carry and leave behind on an otherwise pristine beach. The clamshell had suggested two ways of living life, open or shut. But the sea snail's shell was a spiral, looping in an open-ended circle, a nuanced invitation to stay alert and never to close the door on unexpected opportunities. Ambivalence, certainty. Yes, no, maybe. But in the end, forge ahead.

It must have been that way for her mother, opting to stay in a less than optimal marriage out of duty; yet somehow, her parents had managed to recapture their earlier bonds of love in their old age.

She thought about Christi, her past harmful choices now left behind, moving beyond them to choose reconciliation with Matthew. And she thought about herself – the wavering that preceded the bold choice to leave her marriage, and the miracle of a new life which could not have been imagined, the one that had unfolded because she stayed, at last, true to herself.

During a stroll on the desert during the trip that took her away from all that she had known for nearly twenty years, she heard the sound of a rattler nearby, warning her that danger might lie ahead. Yet, she also spied a shed snakeskin, which suggested a wriggling out of an old life.

Ocotillos sprouted their blazing blooms at the end of spiky stalks, a reminder that, out of thorns, life could blossom with renewed possibilities. In a motel swimming pool, defying an approaching thunderstorm, she had tasted rain droplets as if *she* were the thirsting desert.

She now walked over a wooden footbridge spanning the *acequia*. The muddy water flowed beneath. Russian olives, desert willows and salt cedars still lined the banks of the ditch. But this spot was too open. She would have to find the perfect place.

And then it suddenly hit her. There was no perfect place, no perfect day, no perfect anything, just a progression of time spaces that her emotions identified as vibrantly pleasant or deeply sad. It was enough to return to that less-than-perfect spot and know that bitterness could dissolve, that gratitude could subdue those memories, which, when recalled, left her seared and shaken.

She regretted that she had not spoken to her father about his legacy while he was still alive – that she was his left-behind child, and that she suffered because of it; but also that he gave her, along with her life, another unintended gift. She now recognized what that was – because of his lack of guidance, she acquired the privilege and challenge of carving out her own path to discover her own authentic being. His failure to support the family adequately had left her angry and frustrated. But she now saw that deprivation, in her case, bestowed the ability to feel gratitude for all of life's blessings. She sorely wished she had spoken up on her own behalf, even if such news might have come as a shock to him.

It struck her that sorrow and joy were of the same pattern, just mirror images of one another. Strands of sadness would remain forever woven into the fabric of her being, and she knew that ambivalence held sway in her heart. Before arriving here, she thought she had forgiven her father, but possibly total forgiveness did not come all at once. Healing might arrive in stages. Right now, today, was a first step. The spiral of the seashell found on the dunes and the spiral etched in the dirt under the cottonwood contained a subtle but unmistakable message – stay open to life's potential, regardless of how imperfect it may be.

Stepping slowly away from the bridge, she edged carefully along the top of the bank. At one point, she slipped, then quickly regained her balance. She had a vision of herself becoming the flowing water itself, riding along with its current, carrying away most of the detritus of the past. She felt herself as part of the *all*, floating and emerging, forming new life in a liquid broth, joining in a continuous cycle of birth, life, re-birth, death – rhythmically repeating, steady as a heartbeat.

Descending carefully, walking side-step, moving as close to the water as she dared, she let go of the twig with its green globes, then opened the chest and poured her father's ashes into the steadily moving stream.

Acknowledgments

I am deeply thankful to my circle of readers, who read early drafts of the manuscript and offered encouragement along with constructive suggestions for improvement: Antoinette Roeder, Patricia Cox, Sara Friederich, Robert and Cindy Latham, Julie Holmes, Marsha Willis, and Dr. Linda Leonard. My editor and proofreader, Stephanie Briggs, not only caught typos but also helped sharpen up the language. I also owe a debt of thanks to Pam Knight, able editor and publisher of Plain View Press, for her assistance in bringing this book to publication. Finally, I am so pleased to be able to use as cover art an image of one of the many paintings from the collection of my late husband, Joe Willis. His legacy continues.

Grateful acknowledgment goes to the following for permission to reprint copyrighted material as short quotes used as epigraphs to head chapters or sections:

"The Ninth Elegy," translation copyright © 1982 by Stephen Mitchell; from SELECTED POETRY OF RAINER MARIA RILKE by Rainer Maria Rilke, translated by Stephen Mitchell. Used by permission of Random House, an imprint and division of Penguin Random House LLC. All rights reserved.

Excerpt from LETTER TO MY DAUGHTER by Maya Angelou, copyright © 2008 by Maya Angelou. Used by permission of Random House, an imprint and division of Penguin Random House LLC. All rights reserved.

Excerpt from THE EYE OF THE STORY by Eudora Welty, copyright © 1978 by Eudora Welty. Used by permission of Random House, an imprint and division of Penguin Random House LLC. All rights reserved.

Nancy Key Roeder

Excerpt from THE BLIND ASSASSIN by Margaret Atwood, copyright © 2000 by O.W. Toad, Ltd. Used by permission of Doubleday, an imprint of the Knopf Doubleday Publishing Group, a division of Penguin Random House LLC. All rights reserved.

Biblical quotations are taken from *The Holy Bible*, King James Version.

Various other quotes are deemed to be in fair use or in the public domain, and all work has been credited within the text. Every effort has been made to secure permission to use short quotations, and any omission is inadvertent.

About the Author

Nancy Key Roeder grew up in New Mexico. She began her writing career as a reporter and feature writer for *The Albuquerque Tribune* and continued as a free-lance writer of essays and feature articles published in numerous national and regional publications. A retired teacher, she received a bachelor's degree in English from San Francisco State University and earned a Master of Social Science degree from the University of Colorado at Denver. She is the author of *Going to the Well: A Mother-Daughter Journey* (Plain View Press, 2011).

www.ingramcontent.com/pod-product-compliance
Lightning Source LLC
Chambersburg PA
CBHW030317080526
44584CB00012B/599